Satellite Technology
Second Edition

DATE DUE

MY 21 '02			
AP 1 9 '10			
MR 1 0 '16			

Satellite Technology: An Introduction
Second Edition

A.F. Inglis and A.C. Luther

Focal Press
Boston Oxford Johannesburg Melbourne New Delhi Singapore

Focal Press is an imprint of Butterworth–Heinemann.

…red in a retrieval system, or transmitted in any form or by
recording, or otherwise, without the prior written

…s been written, Butterworth–Heinemann prints its books
on acid-free paper whenever possible.

GLOBAL   Butterworth–Heinemann supports the efforts of American Forests and the Global ReLeaf
RELEAF   program in its campaign for the betterment of trees, forests, and our environment.
2000

Library of Congress Cataloging-in-Publication Data
Inglis, Andrew F.
    Satellite technology : an introduction / A.F. Inglis and A.C.
Luther.—2nd ed.
        p.   cm.
    Includes bibliographical references and index.
    ISBN 0-240-80295-0 (pbk. : alk. paper)
    1. Artificial satellites in telecommunication. 2. Earth stations
(Satellite telecommunication) I. Luther, Arch C. II. Title.
TK5104.I53   1997
384.5'1—dc21   97-14869
                                                       CIP

British Library Cataloguing-in-Publication Data
A catalogue record for this book is available from the British Library.

The publisher offers special discounts on bulk orders of this book.
For information, please contact:
Manager of Special Sales
Butterworth–Heinemann
225 Wildwood Avenue
Woburn, MA 01801–2041
Tel: 617-928-2500
Fax: 617-928-2620

For information on all Focal Press publications available, contact our World Wide Web home page at:
http://www.bh.com/focalpress

10 9 8 7 6 5 4 3

Printed in the United States of America

Contents

Preface to the First Edition

During the past 15 years there has been a phenomenal growth in the use of communication satellites for the transmission and distribution of radio and television programs. Satellites have evolved from a novelty in high technology with an uncertain future, to an indispensable component of these industries. They were initially perceived to be useful mainly for the transmission of voice and data traffic, but as their capabilities became better understood they began to play an equal, if not more important role, in the transmission and distribution of television programs. Later, they became widely used for the distribution of radio programs.

There is now a synergistic relationship between satellites and the radio and television industries. These industries provide a major market for satellite communication services but also are highly dependent on them. Neither cable television (CATV) nor electronic news gathering (ENG) could have reached its present state of development without the use of satellites.

The introduction of satellites into the radio and television industries created a new set of challenges and opportunities for the members of their technical communities. The new concepts, new vocabulary, and new technologies of satellites must be learned by the engineers responsible for the design and operation of broadcasting and cable TV systems. It is equally a requirement for students who are pursuing a course of study leading to employment in the engineering departments of broadcasting and cable TV companies.

This volume contributes to the learning process by providing an introduction to satellite technology in language that is accessible to those who are not specialists. The scope of its subject matter is broad, ranging from the theory of satellite operation to practical instructions for the initial setup of mobile earth stations. For those who wish to pursue the study of the technical aspects of satellites further, a comprehensive list of references are included.

The author is indebted to the many members of the broadcasting and satellite industries who supplied reference materials and invaluable advice and suggestions. He is grateful to Wayne Rawlings and his staff from Station KCRA-TV in Sacramento who provided information on the practical operation of satellite news gathering (SNG) earth stations. Most of all he wishes to thank Walter Braun, John Christopher, and Marvin Freeling of GE American Communications. They were an indispensable resource, and they carefully reviewed the manuscript for technical accuracy. Any remaining errors, however, are the author's!

Preface to the Second Edition

The satellite communications industry and its customers have not stood still in the seven years since the writing of the First Edition of this book. In fact, major expansion and major changes have occurred. Not the least of these is the maturation of digital television and the digital direct-to-home satellite broadcasting services. These alone justify this Second Edition.

Satellite design technology has also advanced to allow larger, higher-powered satellites to be built and put into operation economically.

The authorship of this book also has changed. Andrew F. Inglis is in the process of retiring fully from writing and he has asked his friend, Arch C. Luther, who is an experienced writer (seven books) to join as co-author. Arch is largely responsible for the production of this Second Edition.

As with any project like this, the authors depend on others for sources of information, review, comments, and encouragement. For this Second Edition, we must acknowledge the help of Walter Braun and Dany Harel of GE Americom.

1

Satellite Communication Systems

1.1 INTRODUCTION

Communication of electrical signals is done by direct physical connection, such as wires or fiber-optic cables, or by radiation of radio frequency (RF) or optical waves. In radiated communication, the use of satellites for relaying signals has significant advantages in certain applications. In order to send signals between points on the earth's surface, the signal is radiated up to a satellite in orbit and then relayed back down to earth where it is received at a different location. Such technology is widely used in telephony, data communication, and communication of radio and television signals in many applications. This book focuses on the use of satellite communication for radio and television signals.

This chapter is an overview of the technology of satellite communication systems used for the transmission and distribution of radio and television programs. Succeeding chapters describe the applications and technical characteristics of satellites and earth stations, earth station equipment and design procedures, Federal Communications Commission (FCC) rules and regulations, earth station installation and operational procedures, and sources of satellite services and equipment.

1.1.1 Satellite Communication System Elements

The elements of a satellite communication system are shown in Figure 1.1.

The signals to be transmitted, that is, the *baseband signals,* are delivered to an *uplink earth station,* where they modulate a high-power radio frequency transmitter. The earth station antenna radiates the transmitter's signal to a *geosynchronous* satellite, which appears to remain in a fixed position in space relative to the earth's surface. The satellite receives the radiated signal, shifts its frequency, and amplifies it by means of a *transponder,* then reradiates it to back to earth where it can be received by *downlink* earth stations in the coverage area of the satellite.

Earth stations form the *ground segment* of a satellite communication system, while the satellite constitutes the *space segment.* The transmission system from earth station to satellite is called an uplink, and the system from satellite to earth is called a downlink.

1

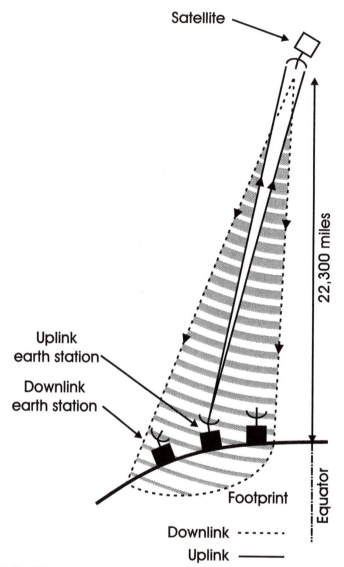

Figure 1.1 Satellite communication system.

1.1.2 Satellite Service Areas

Earth station antennas have very narrow beams, both to increase their gain and to avoid interference with adjacent satellites. By contrast, the antennas on communication satellites usually have rather broad beams so that they can provide service to and from a large area—typically an entire region, country, or even an entire hemisphere. In an exception to this practice, some satellites have narrow *spot beams* for specialized service to limited areas. The area on the earth's surface that receives a signal of useful strength from the satellite is known as its *footprint*.

1.1.3 Satellite Frequency Bands

Two frequency bands, C band (3.4 to 7.0 GHz) and Ku band (10.7 to 15.0 GHz) are used for satellite transmission of radio and television programs. C-band downlink transmissions are in the 4 GHz region of the spectrum, which is shared with terrestrial microwave services. The sharing causes limitation of the power and location of some C-band satellite systems. Ku-band downlinks operate in the 12 GHz region and have exclusive use of these frequencies. Direct Broadcast Satellite (DBS) downlinks operate in the 12.5 GHz region and are intended for direct pickup by small home antennas. The technical characteristics of these frequency bands are described in Section 3.1.2.1.

1.1.4 Transmission Modes

Radio-frequency transmission requires that the baseband signal be modulated on a carrier in the desired frequency band. There are three options that are widely used for radio and television transmission—analog amplitude modulation (AM), analog frequency modulation (FM), and digital modulation.

1.1.4.1 AM Transmission

Terrestrial television broadcasting is almost exclusively based on AM. This is the simplest type of modulation from the viewpoint of both transmitter and receiver. However, it depends critically on a linear amplitude transfer characteristic and it is not appropriate for channels that have inherent nonlinearities.

1.1.4.2 FM Transmission

Frequency modulation is well suited for the transmission of television signals, and it has been almost universally used in satellites until recently, when digital modulation methods have come into use. Compared to other analog modulation methods, FM has three important advantages for this purpose:

1. It does not require highly linear power amplifiers, either in the satellite or the uplink.
2. It has a substantial *noise improvement factor* (see Chapters 4 and 5), so that the signal-to-noise-ratio (SNR) of the output video signal is higher than that of the radio frequency carrier.
3. The transmitted energy can be more uniformly distributed across the channel bandwidth by *sideband energy dispersal*. This process is important for C-band systems because it increases the legally permissible downlink power (see Chapter 4).

Properly designed FM transmission systems provide high performance and have been the backbone of satellite communication since the first communication satellite went up. However, the wave of the future is digital transmission.

1.1.4.3 Digital Transmission

For digital transmission, an audio or video signal is first converted to a stream of digital bits by *analog-to-digital conversion* (ADC). Once in digital form, the signal is processed by digital circuits to provide features such as data reduction (called *compression*) or to provide for the correction of transmission errors (called *error protection*). These processes allow digital transmissions to operate in less bandwidth than equivalent-performing FM systems and to provide essentially noise-free transmission. Because of this, most new communication systems employ digital technology.

Digital transmission was first applied to high-fidelity audio signals, and it is widely used by radio networks for program distribution (see Chapters 2 and 5). Digital transmission of television signals, which requires higher data rates and more complex digital processing, is a more recent development that is now seeing widespread use with the Direct Broadcast Satellite (DBS) systems (see Section 2.5).

Digital transmission can actually *reduce* the bandwidth required for a video signal transmission system, a feature that results from the repetitiveness and large amount of redundancy in the video signal. Digital processing techniques can *compress* the video data to achieve data rates that allow several high-quality digital TV channels to be transmitted in the same bandwidth as a single analog FM TV signal.

The worldwide HDTV initiatives have all focused on digital transmission for future advanced television (ATV) systems. The United States has recently decided on such a system that will be deployed in the next several years for terrestrial broadcasting. It will offer a choice of resolution levels ranging from present "standard" definition (SDTV) to full high-definition TV (HDTV), and it is transmitted digitally in a standard 6 MHz television channel for terrestrial broadcasting. This system can be transmitted over existing satellite communication facilities.

1.1.5 Competitive Transmission Mediums

For the transmission of television signals, satellites compete with other communication mediums—microwave, coaxial cable, and fiber-optic cable. Each of these mediums has characteristics which make it especially suited for certain types of service. None of them excels in all respects, and all will continue to be used extensively in the foreseeable future.

To date, the competition to satellites for television service has come primarily from coaxial cable and microwave. Fiber optics is now coming into use and will significantly change the competitive situation in the future.

The most striking feature of fiber-optic systems is their enormous bandwidth—a typical system has a bandwidth of 3 GHz (3,000 MHz) as compared with 36 MHz for a single satellite transponder or 864 MHz for the 24 transponders in a C-band satellite. Fiber-optic systems generally use digital transmission, so they are ideal for the digital video techniques that have been developed.

Fiber-optic cable systems are being installed for intercity, point-to-point transmission circuits by all major communication carriers for voice, data, and video. These facilities will doubtless provide serious competition to satellites for fixed, point-to-point video transmission services.

1.1.6 The Information Superhighway

Long-range planners in the communications industry envision a future that goes beyond fixed point-to-point services. A concept called the *information superhighway* (ISH) would provide every home and business with a high data-rate digital connection to a nationwide communication system. Two-way digital bit streams on the system would provide radio and television programs, telephone service, facsimile service, and access to remotely located computers and a variety of data banks to every home and business. Both satellites and fiber-optic cable are possibilities for implementing such a system.

The data architecture of the ISH would be like the present-day Internet, which is a worldwide network of computers providing data for public access. Except for major business or academic sites, most people access the Internet using analog telephone lines, which limits them to data rates in the range of 30,000 bits/second. Such a low rate is not usable for real time television but the Internet still demonstrates the use of a worldwide digital network for information transfer and communication and it is widely used. When an ISH connection is available to everyone with data rates above 1,000,000 bits/second (1 Mb/s), the ISH can become a viable video carrier.

The ISH is an extremely attractive concept but the installation and operation of such a nationwide system involves massive technical, financial, and political problems, not all of which yet have clear solutions. It could well be more than a decade before such a system is designed, approved by the government, financed, constructed, and put into operation.

1.2 SATELLITE ORBITS

There are three classes of orbits for communication satellites:

Low earth orbit (LEO)—500 to 900 km altitude

Medium earth orbit (MEO)—5,000 to 12,000 km altitude

Geosynchronous orbit (GEO)—36,000 km altitude

In both LEO and MEO orbits, the satellite moves with respect to the surface of the earth and a system for continuous communication requires multiple satellites in orbit so that at least one will always be in view. Even so, communication systems are being designed for LEO or MEO satellites although none has yet been deployed.

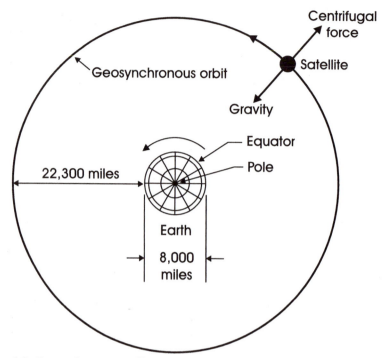

Figure 1.2 Geosynchronous satellites.

1.2.1 Geosynchronous Location

The geosynchronous orbit (GEO) places the satellite at an altitude where it appears stationary from the earth's surface. All communication satellite systems to date use GEO orbits. The discussion in the rest of this section applies only to GEO satellites.

GEO satellites are located in the *geosynchronous orbit,* which forms a circle in the plane of the equator, 35,785 km (22,300 miles) above the earth (see Figure 1.2). They revolve once each day in synchronism with the earth's rotation; and at this elevation the gravitational force pulling them toward the earth is exactly balanced by the centrifugal force pulling them outward. Since GEO satellites revolve at the same rotational speed as the earth, they appear stationary from the earth's surface; and radio signals can be transmitted to and from them with highly directional antennas pointed in a fixed direction. This is the property that makes satellite communications practical with a single satellite.

The distance of a GEO satellite above the earth causes a propagation delay of 0.25 second for a round trip up to the satellite and back to earth. This is a factor in some applications such as the ISH. Propagation delay is one area where systems based on MEO or LEO satellites have an obvious advantage. However, delay does not matter to radio or television distribution systems.

1.2.2 Orbital Slots

International regulatory bodies and national governmental organizations, such as the Federal Communications Commission (FCC) in the United States (see Chapter 6), designate the locations on the geosynchronous orbit where communication satellites can be placed. These locations are specified in degrees of longitude and are known as *orbital slots*.

Since all communication satellites operate in the same frequency bands, the spacing between orbital slots must be great enough to reduce, to an acceptable level, the interference between transmissions to and from adjacent satellites. The minimum spacing required to achieve this objective depends on the width of the earth station antenna beams, that is, the directivity of their antennas.

In response to the huge demand for orbital slots, the FCC has progressively reduced the required spacing and has established a future standard of only 2° for C- and Ku-band satellites—a spacing which requires the use of very narrow antenna beams. However, DBS satellites are designed to be received by smaller and less directional receiving antennas in individual homes (see Chapter 4 for the relation between antenna size and beam width). Accordingly, DBS orbital slot assignments are located at intervals of 9°.

1.2.3 Western Hemisphere Orbital Slot Allocations and Assignments

By international agreement negotiated through the International Telecommunications Union (ITU), each country is allocated an arc of the geosynchronous orbit, within which it can assign orbital slots. A national regulatory body—the FCC in the case of the United States—makes the slot assignments within this arc. The current (1997) orbital slot allocations and assignments for the western hemisphere are tabulated on the following pages. Fixed service satellites (FSS) provide point-to-point communication between fixed, non-mobile, locations, and direct broadcast satellites (DBS) provide broadcast service to homes and other users. The slot assignments change frequently, so the tables should be viewed as an early 1997 snapshot.

1.2.3.1 United States

The United States is allocated the orbital arcs 62° to 103° and 120° to 146° west longitude for C-band satellites and 62° to 105° and 120° to 136° west longitude for Ku-band satellites. Within each band, a single satellite is assigned to each slot. The assignments as of 1997 within these arcs are shown in Table 1.1 and Figure 1.3.

The United States is also allocated the eight DBS slots in the arc 62° to 175°, listed in Table 1.1. The power requirements of DBS satellites are so great that it is not always practical to provide power in a single satellite for all the channels in a single slot. Accordingly, more than one satellite is assigned to each slot; and channels rather than satellites are assigned to individual applicants. Up to 32 channels per slot may be assigned. Current DBS slot assignments are listed in Table 2.2.

Table 1.1 United States Orbital Slot Assignments—1997

C-band Fixed Service Satellites (FSS)

W.Long.	*Name*	*Operator*
69°	Spacenet 2 (hybrid)	GE Americom
74°	Galaxy VI	Hughes
85°	GE-2 (hybrid)	GE Americom
87°	Spacenet 3R (hybrid)	GE Americom
89°	Telstar 402R (hybrid)	AT&T
91°	Galaxy VII (hybrid)	Hughes
95°	Galaxy IIIR (hybrid)	Hughes
99°	Galaxy IV (hybrid)	Hughes
101°	Spacenet 4 (hybrid)	Contel ASC
103°	GE-1 (hybrid)	GE Americom
123°	Galaxy IX	Hughes
125°	Galaxy V	Hughes
131°	Satcom C3	GE Americom
133°	Galaxy IR (hybrid)	Hughes
135°	Satcom C4	GE Americom
137°	Satcom C1	GE Americom
139°	Satcom C5	GE Americom

Ku-band Fixed Service Satellites (FSS)

69°	Spacenet 2 (hybrid)	GE Americom
74°	SBS-6	Hughes
77°	SBS-4	Hughes
85°	Satcom K2	GE Americom
85°	GE-2 (hybrid)	GE Americom
87°	Spacenet 3R (hybrid)	GE Americom
89°	Telstar 402R (hybrid)	AT&T
91°	Galaxy VII (hybrid)	IBM
95°	Galaxy IIIR (hybrid)	Hughes
99°	Galaxy IV (hybrid)	Hughes
101°	Spacenet 4 (hybrid)	GE Americom
103°	GE-1 (hybrid)	GE Americom
105°	Gstar 4	GE Americom
123°	SBS-5	Hughes
125°	Gstar 2	GE Americom
133°	Galaxy IR (hybrid)	Hughes

Table 1.1 United States Orbital Slot Assignments—1997 (continued)

Ku-band Direct Broadcast Satellites (DBS)

61.5°	
101.0°	See Table 2.2 for channel
110.0°	assignments within these
119.0°	slots.
148.0°	
157.0°	These slots were originally intended for coverage of western
166.0°	CONUS. With high-powered DBS satellites, CONUS is covered
175.0°	entirely by the more easterly slots above. These slots are unused.

Source: http://www.sat-net.com/pck/positions/east2west.htm.

1.2.3.2 Canada

Canadian satellites are located in the arc 104.5°-117.5° west longitude. Canadian satellites in orbit as of 1997 are shown in Table 1.2.

1.2.3.3 Mexico and South America

Mexico shares orbital slots with Canada. Because of their geographic separation, satellites can operate in the same frequency band and from the same slot without excessive interference.

South America shares orbital slots with the United States. The South American continent lies somewhat to the east of North America; and South American countries utilize an arc that partially overlaps the U.S. arc but extends to the east of it. Orbital slots assigned to Mexico and South America as of 1997 are shown in Table 1.3.

1.2.4 Satellite Look, or Elevation Angle

The *look* angle, the elevation of the path to the satellite above the horizontal, is critical to the performance of its transmission link. Three problems are encountered with low elevation angles that are just above the horizon:

1. Difficulty in clearing buildings, trees, and other terrestrial objects—failure of the path to do so may result in attenuation of the signal by absorption or in distortions from multipath reflections.
2. Atmospheric attenuation—the length of a low elevation path through the atmosphere before it emerges into space is much longer; and this increases rain attenuation, particularly when operating in the Ku band.

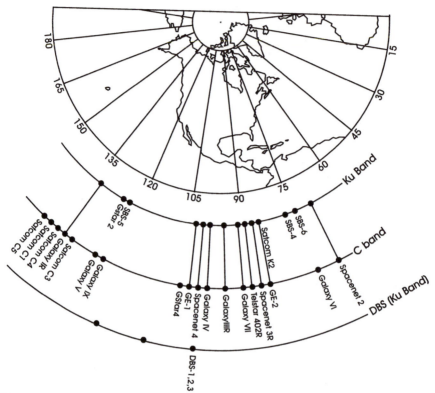

Figure 1.3 United States orbital slot assignments.

Table 1.2 Canadian Orbital Slot Assignments—1997

C-band Fixed Service Satellites (FSS)

W. Long.	_Name_	_Operator_
107.3°	Anik E2 (hybrid)	Telsat Canada
111.1°	Anik E1 (hybrid)	Telsat Canada

Ku-band, Fixed Satellite Service (FSS)

107.3°	Anik E2 (hybrid)	Telsat Canada
109.2°	Nahuel 2 (Anik C2)	Paracom S. A.
109.3°	Nahuel 1 (Anik C1)	Paracom S. A.
111.1°	Anik E1 (hybrid)	Telsat Canada
114.9°	Anik C3	Telsat Canada

Source: http://www.sat-net.com/pck/positions/east2west.htm.

Table 1.3 Mexican and South American Orbital Slot Assignments—1996

Hybrid C- and Ku-band Fixed Service Satellites (FSS)

MEXICO

W.Long.	*Name*
109.2°	Solidaridad 1
113°	Solidaridad 2
116.8°	Morelos 2

SOUTH AMERICA

Country or orbital administration	*Slot*	*Satellite*	*Frequency*
Argentina	80.0°	Nahuel 1	C/Ku-band
	85.0°	Nahuel 2	C/Ku-band
Brazil	61.0°	SBTS B3	C-band
	61.0°	SBTS C3	Ku-band
	65.0°	Brasilsat B2	C-band
	65.0°	SBTS A2	C-band
	65.0°	SBTS B2	C-band
	65.0°	SBTS C2	Ku-band
	70.0°	Brasilsat B1	C-band
	70.0°	SBTS A1	C-band
	92.0°	SBTS A2	C-band
Colombia	75.0°	Colombia 2	C-band
	75.0°	Satcol 2	C-band
	75.4°	Colombia 1A	C-band
	75.4°	Satcol 1A	C-band
	75.4°	Satcol 2B	C-band
Cuba	83.0°	STSC 1	C-band
	97.0°	STSC 2	C-band
ASETA	72.0°	Simon Bolivar C	C-band
(Bolivia, Ecuador,	77.5°	Simon Bolivar A	C-band
Peru, Venezuela)	89.0°	Simon Bolivar B	C-band
	106.0°	Simon Bolivar 1	C-band

Source: http://www.sat-net.com/pck/positions/east2west.htm

3. Electrical noise generated by the earth's heat near its surface—this noise is picked up by the side lobes of receiving antennas aimed along a low-elevation path, and the SNR of the link is adversely affected.

For downlinks, it is current design practice to utilize a minimum elevation angle of 5° for C-band satellites and 10° to 20° for K-band (see Chapter 4). For uplinks, the FCC requires a minimum elevation angle of 5° for all frequency bands, with possible exceptions for seaward paths where permission may be given for elevation angles as low as 3° (see Para. 25.505 of Part 25 of the FCC Rules).

1.2.5 The Prime Orbital Arcs

Because of the problems of transmission paths with low elevation angles, some orbital slots are more desirable than others. The orbital slot should be at a location which will result in a minimum elevation angle of 5° for C band and 10° to 20° for Ku band, for antennas located anywhere in the desired service area. The portions of the geosynchronous orbit in which the slots meet this condition are called *prime orbital arcs*.

The limits of the prime orbital arcs for 5° horizon clearance (C band) in the continental United States (CONUS) and selected points in Hawaii and Alaska are as follows:

	Degrees west longitude
CONUS	55-138
CONUS, plus Hawaii	80-138
CONUS, plus Anchorage	88-138
North Slope (Alaska)	120-190

The prime arcs for Ku band are shorter because of the need for greater elevation angles. When earth stations are operated at northerly latitudes, the prime arcs are comparatively short, as shown in the previous table. Antenna elevation angles are low throughout Alaska, and satellites are below the horizon at the north pole.

1.2.6 Solar Eclipses

Solar eclipses occur when the earth comes between the sun and the satellite. They are not of direct interest to the users of satellite services, but they have a major effect on satellite design. The satellite depends on solar energy to provide electrical power to all of its systems, and this energy source is interrupted when the sun is eclipsed by the earth. Eclipses occur near midnight at the satellite's longitude for 21 days before and after each equinox, and their duration reaches a maximum of 72 minutes at the equinox. Batteries are installed on board the satellite to maintain a source of power during the eclipse period.

1.2.7 Sun Outages

The elevated temperature of the sun causes it to transmit a high-level electrical noise signal to receiving systems whenever it passes behind the satellite and comes within the beams of the receiver antennas. The increase in noise is so severe that a signal outage usually results. The length and number of the outages depends on the latitude of the earth station and the diameter of the antenna. At an average latitude of 40° in the continental United States, and a 10-meter antenna, the outages occur over 6 days with a maximum duration of 8 minutes each day. With a less directional 3-meter antenna, the outages occur over 15 days, with a maximum duration of 24 minutes.

The times and durations of sun outages can be calculated precisely,[1] but this requires the use of astronomical tables that are frequently not available in the broadcasting industry. An easier way is to obtain the information from the satellite carriers, all of which have developed computer programs for outage calculations.

There is no way of avoiding sun outages; and if continuous service must be maintained, the only solution is to switch temporarily to another satellite.

1.3 SATELLITE LAUNCHING

Although users of satellite communication services are not directly concerned with satellite launching, it is useful for them to have a general knowledge of the process.

Placing the satellite in the geosynchronous orbit, 22,300 miles above the earth, requires an enormous amount of energy; and it probably would not have been possible were it not for the advances in rocketry that resulted from government military and scientific programs.

The launch process can be divided into two phases, namely, the *launch phase* and the *orbit injection phase.* During the launch phase, the *launch vehicle* places the satellite in a *transfer orbit*—an elliptical orbit that at its highest point, the *apogee,* is at the geosynchronous elevation of 22,300 miles and at its lowest point, the *perigee,* is at an elevation usually not less than 100 miles.

When a satellite is launched from the earth's surface, it inherently enters an orbit whose plane has an inclination equal to the latitude of the launch site. For example, satellites launched from the Kennedy Space Center in Florida will have an orbital inclination of 28°. To achieve the desired equatorial orbit (inclination = 0°), the inclination must be corrected in the process of moving from the transfer orbit to the final orbit. This requires additional energy. The inclination-change energy requirement can be reduced by using a supersynchronous transfer orbit, where the perigee elevation is substantially greater that the geosynchronous elevation. It can be shown that this reduces the energy required in the satellite for achieving the final orbit.

The energy required to raise the satellite from the elliptical transfer orbit to the circular geosynchronous orbit is supplied by a thruster on the satellite. One approach is the *apogee kick motor* (AKM), which is a solid-fuel rocket that is fired once to place the satellite into its final geosynchronous orbit. The one-shot aspect of the AKM has caused the loss of some satellites when the firing did not go exactly right. More recently, a liquid-fueled engine that can be fired repeatedly under ground control has been used. This is called a *liquid apogee engine* (LAE) and it allows the orbiting process to be accomplished in small steps with careful monitoring and control from the ground at each stage.

There are two types of launch vehicles: *expendable rockets,* which are destroyed while completing their mission, and the *space shuttle* (more formally called the *space transportation system* or STS), which is reusable.

1.3.1 Expendable Rockets

Expendable rockets for communication satellites have multiple stages that allow the rocket to drop off the weight of stages as they are used up. A typical expendable rocket will have three stages.

The first stage contains several hundred thousand pounds of a kerosene/liquid-oxygen mixture, plus a number of solid fuel rocket boosters that produce a tremendous display of flame—and ear-splitting noise—as the satellite lifts off its pad. It raises the satellite to an elevation of about 50 miles. The second stage raises the satellite to 100 miles, and the third stage places it in the transfer orbit.

After the satellite is placed in its transfer orbit, the rocket's mission is complete, and its remnants fall to earth. The satellite is placed in its final geosynchronous orbital slot by the AKM, which is fired on-command while the satellite is at the apogee of the transfer orbit.

1.3.2 The Space Shuttle

The Space Shuttle, or Space Transportation System (STS), performs the functions of the first two stages of an expendable launch vehicle. The satellite—together with the third stage, variously called an IUS (Integrated Upper Stage), SSUS (Spin Stabilized Upper Stage), or a PAM (Payload Assist Module)—are mounted in the cargo bay of the shuttle. When the shuttle reaches its orbital elevation of 150 to 200 miles, the satellite and third stage are ejected from the cargo compartment. The third stage is fired, placing the satellite in the transfer orbit. The AKM in the satellite then places it in the geosynchronous orbit.

After all of its cargo has been jettisoned, the shuttle returns to earth for refurbishing and reuse.

1.3.3 History and Current Status of Launch Vehicles

All communication satellites launched from 1975 to 1982 used expendable rockets. In the early 1980s, the National Aeronautics and Space Administration (NASA) decided to abandon rockets and to move to the space shuttle. The space shuttle was designed to have the capability of putting very heavy satellites into orbit at a relatively low cost—the low cost resulting from the shuttle's reusability. Although development of the space shuttle was marked by serious technical difficulties, NASA was sufficiently confident of the shuttle's performance to cease taking reservations for expendable vehicle launches that would occur after 1984. Unfortunately, the technical problems were not solved on a timely basis; and they came to a climax with the tragic Challenger failure on January 28, 1986. At that time, only four commercial satellites (SBS, Telsat Canada, and GE Americom K1 and K2) had been shuttle-launched.

The defects in the space shuttle design, which were highlighted by the Challenger disaster, soon brought launches of commercial satellites by United States vehicles to a halt. Production of suitable expendable vehicles had virtually ceased, and lengthy engineering programs were required to solve the problems in the shuttle.

For a time, the Ariane rocket, a product of the European Space Agency (ESA), was the only available rocket for commercial satellites. ESA launched 7 United States satellites between 1984 and 1988, and 4 additional launches were scheduled for 1990.

In August 1986, a presidential directive was issued requiring the phaseout of the launch of commercial satellites by the government, and the reservation of the shuttle for scientific and military payloads. As a result, the shuttle is no longer used for launch of commercial satellites.

NASA and Air Force launch *facilities,* however, were made available to private companies; and contracts were negotiated with McDonnell Douglas (Delta rocket), General Dynamics (Atlas rocket), and Martin Marietta (Titan rocket) for the use of facilities in Florida and California. The first launch (an Italian satellite) under this program occurred in August 1989 with a Delta rocket. The McDonnell Douglas Delta series has the best record for commercial satellite launching.

1.4 COMMUNICATION SATELLITES

A communications satellite has two basic elements, the *platform,* or *bus,* and the communications *payload.*

1.4.1 The Satellite Bus

As suggested by its name, the purpose of the bus is to provide a working environment for the payload, while maintaining it in its orbital slot. The bus includes the mechanical housing for the satellite, and the *housekeeping* systems that include primary power for all electrical and electronic components; thermal control to maintain on-board temperatures; tracking, telemetry, and control systems (TT&C), which includes the *station keeping* facilities to maintain satellite orbital location and attitude.

1.4.2 The Payload

The payload consists of the communication system components (see Chapter 3). They include the antennas, receivers, and transponders. The payload is the reason for existence of the satellite and is what the customer pays for.

1.5 EARTH STATIONS

1.5.1 Earth Station Types

Earth stations vary widely in complexity and cost. At one extreme are the TVROs (television, receive only), that are used by individual homeowners. C-band earth stations used by homeowners are called *backyard dishes* and may be purchased for less than $2,000. DBS earth stations for homes can cost less than $500. The earth stations employed by major satellite carriers are at the other extreme. They may include:

1. a number of very large antennas for communicating with several satellites simultaneously;
2. precision systems for tracking satellites;
3. uplink and downlink communication equipment; and
4. TT&C (tracking, telemetry, and control) systems for monitoring the performance of the satellites and maintaining them in the correct attitude in their orbital slots (station keeping). They are equipped with elaborate backup systems to provide a high degree of reliability, and their cost is measured in millions of dollars.

A description of the design and operation of the costly and complex earth stations employed by major satellite carriers is beyond the scope of this volume.[2] However, earth stations used by television broadcasting stations, major television networks, specialized and *ad hoc* television networks, cable TV systems, television program suppliers, and home viewers are covered in this book. The equipment used in these earth stations are described in Chapter 4 and their system design is described in Chapter 5.

1.5.2 Uplink Earth Stations

A block diagram of a typical uplink earth station is shown in Figure 1.4.

If scrambling is employed to prevent unauthorized reception, the video and audio signals first pass through the *scrambler*. The scrambled signals are then fed to the *signal processor*, the heart of the uplink earth station (Section 4.2 provides more information about signal processing). The signal processor performs the processes required by the modulation method (see Section 1.1.4) of the system and delivers its output modulated on a convenient *intermediate frequency* (IF). This goes to the upconverter unit, which converts the IF signal to the final carrier frequency and amplifies it to a higher level. The output of the upconverter is fed to a *high-power amplifier (HPA),* which is connected by waveguide to the antenna that radiates the signal to the satellite.

1.5.3 Downlink Earth Stations

A block diagram of a typical downlink earth station is shown in Figure 1.5.

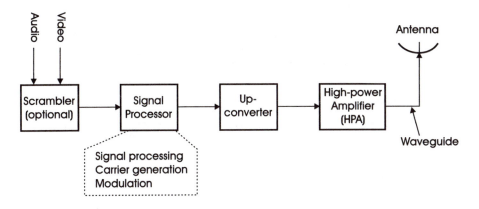

Figure 1.4 Block diagram of a typical uplink earth station.

The antenna receives the signal from the satellite and feeds it to a *low-noise amplifier (LNA)*, which provides the initial amplification. The output of the LNA is then fed to the receiver at the original carrier frequency through a waveguide. Alternatively, a *low-noise block downconverter (LNB)*, can be used, which translates all of the satellite's carrier frequencies of the same polarization to the first IF frequency, usually 950 to 1450 MHz in the L band. This permits the connection from the antenna to the receiver to be made through a coaxial cable rather than a waveguide.

In an alternative configuration, only the LNA is mounted at the antenna; and its output, still at the original carrier frequency, is fed to the downconverter at the receiver by waveguide.

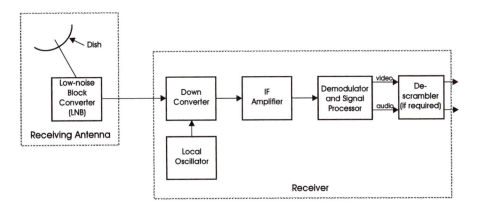

Figure 1.5 Block diagram of a typical downlink earth station.

The antenna gain and the quality of the LNA are the key receiver components in determining its most basic performance specification, the SNR. The quality of commercial LNA amplifiers varies widely in accordance with their cost. The difference in noise performance of a cryogenically cooled LNA in a major earth station and an inexpensive backyard-dish LNA may be 10 dB or more.

1.6 SUMMARY

A satellite communication system has two major components, the earth segment and the space segment The earth segment includes (1) an uplink earth station that transmits a signal to the satellite and (2) a downlink earth station that receives and amplifies the signal transmitted back to earth by the satellite. The space segment is the satellite itself. It includes a number of transponders, each tuned to a single channel from the uplink. The transponder amplifies the signal and retransmits it to earth at a different frequency.

Launching a satellite into a geosynchronous orbit, 22,300 miles above the earth, is a major technical feat The original launches of geosynchronous satellites employed expendable launch vehicles, that is, rockets. As a matter of government policy, the space shuttle was employed for a time; but a series of technical problems with the shuttle have caused the industry to revert to rockets for launching commercial satellites.

During the last two decades, the uses of satellites have expanded from intelligence gathering, military, and scientific, to include important commercial applications, including the transmission and distribution of radio and television programs, as described in Chapter 2.

Notes

1   See Loeffler, John, "Planning for Solar Outages," *Satellite Communications,* April 1983.

2   See bibliography for references.

2

Satellites in Radio and Television

2.1 THE UNIQUE ADVANTAGES OF SATELLITES

The importance of satellites to the radio and television industries is based on three unique characteristics:

1. The cost of satellite circuits is independent of their length—a signal can be transmitted by satellite across the country or across the ocean as cheaply as across the street. This makes satellite transmission cost competitive for some long-haul, point-to-point circuits within the United States; and, given the current limits on the bandwidth and capacity of undersea cables, it has been indispensable for transoceanic television circuits.

2. Downlink signals can be received over a wide area, a property which makes satellites a particularly cost effective and flexible medium for point-to-multipoint program distribution to cable TV systems, broadcast network affiliates, and to private homes.

3. Since uplink signals can originate over a wide area, satellites are useful or even indispensable for temporary communication circuits originating from mobile earth stations, particularly those which must be established on short notice, as in satellite news gathering (SNG).[1]

2.2 DEREGULATION

The usage of satellites for television and radio program transmission has been greatly increased by the policy of deregulation that the FCC has followed in recent years, particularly with respect to rates and earth station rules.

2.2.1 Rates

The first generation satellite communication companies—namely, AT&T, RCA, and Western Union—initially offered their services on a common carrier basis with all the restrictions of that mode. The FCC did not require common carrier operation, but it required carriers to file tariffs, and carriers were subject to rate regulation. Subsequently, the rates and other commercial policies of satellite carriers have become almost completely deregulated; and satellite users can now obtain services through a wide variety of sale and lease arrangements.

2.2.2 Receive-Only Earth Stations

The deregulation of receive-only earth stations in 1979 has had an even more striking effect on the usage of satellites.

FCC Rules originally required these stations to have a minimum antenna diameter of 10 meters, and to be licensed. To obtain a license, the applicant had to make a showing that the proposed site was *clear,* that is, that it did not receive objectionable interference from existing microwave systems or satellite uplinks. With these restrictions, the cost of typical receive-only earth stations used by cable TV systems was $75,000.

The requirements for minimum antenna diameter and licensing were eliminated in 1979. Most cable systems now use 5-meter antennas, and the size reduction—together with price competition and economies of scale—have reduced the cost of cable system earth stations to $5000 or less. Backyard-dish earth stations with less demanding performance requirements can be obtained for less than $2000 and DBS earth stations cost less that $500.

Obtaining a license is now optional for receive-only earth stations. A licensed receive-only earth station has the advantage of being protected against interference from future microwave and satellite systems.

Satellites and uplink earth stations continue to be subject to technical regulation (see Chapter 6). Its purpose is to prevent or minimize interference between satellites, between satellites and microwave systems, and between users of the same satellite. It is also intended to maximize the usage of the spectrum.

2.3 SATELLITE USAGE BY CABLE TV SYSTEMS

The distribution of programs to cable TV systems was the first major use of satellites by the television industry; and cable program suppliers continue to be one of the largest markets for satellite services. It is a synergistic relationship because satellite program distribution is responsible for the extraordinary growth of the cable TV industry.

2.3.1 History

In the pre-satellite era, the programming for cable TV systems was limited to off-the-air pickups from nearby broadcast stations and to programs imported by microwave from more distant stations. The variety of programs available to cable subscribers in the more populous metropolitan areas was not much greater than could be received off-the-air from local stations; and cable had little appeal in these areas. By 1977, the end of the pre-satellite era, the number of cable TV subscribers had grown to about 12 million, but the prospects for further growth were not encouraging.

Satellite distribution of cable TV program services came into being in 1977; and cable systems were able to offer attractive programs which were not available from broadcast stations, even in the largest cities. With this incentive, the number of cable systems and the number of subscribers grew rapidly. In 1996, the number of subscribers was more than 60 million.

This growth was aided by the deregulation of the receive-only earth stations used by cable systems (see earlier discussion in this Chapter). Before deregulation, the $75,000 price tag for 10-meter earth stations was beyond the means of smaller cable systems. It was almost mandatory to group all program services on a single satellite so that they could be received with a single antenna. The licensing process was costly and time consuming; and it was sometimes impossible to get clearance for head-end sites where the earth station could be located—in accordance with the FCC's rigid interference standards.

With deregulation in 1979, these barriers were removed. Earth station prices came down rapidly, multiple-satellite transmission of different program services became practical, and the number of available services was no longer limited to the capacity of a single satellite.

2.3.2 Satellite-Distributed Cable TV Program Services

Three types of program services, namely, basic, pay, and pay-per-view, are distributed to cable TV systems by satellite.

Basic services are provided by cable TV systems to their subscribers for a flat monthly fee. They include both off-the-air broadcast programs and programs distributed by satellite. Suppliers of basic services receive revenue by some combination of advertising and a small monthly per-subscriber charge to the cable system operator.

Pay or premium services are available to subscribers for the payment of an additional monthly fee, which is shared by the cable operator and the program supplier.

Pay-per-view services are available to subscribers for the payment of a fee for each program viewed. Both pay and pay-per-view require a means of controlling the access to these channels on an individual-subscriber basis. On cable systems, this is handled by the hardware provided to the subscriber.

2.3.3 Scrambling

The reduction in earth station prices had an unexpected effect: the unauthorized pirating of satellite signals intended for cable TV systems by the use of *backyard dishes,* that is, low-cost C-band receive-only earth stations installed by members of the public. This led to the necessity of scrambling the signals of pay-TV services to prevent their reception except by authorized earth stations. (See Sections 2.5.6 and 4.2 for further discussion of scrambling systems.)

2.4 SATELLITE USAGE BY TELEVISION BROADCASTING

The television broadcasting industry adopted satellite program distribution more slowly than cable TV, but it has since become an integral part of the broadcasting medium. Most broadcast stations now have several earth stations that are used for the reception of network and syndicated programs and for the transmission and reception of news and sports programs from remote locations.

2.4.1 Public Broadcasting Service (PBS)

The Public Broadcasting Service (PBS) was the first major broadcasting organization to make extensive use of satellite program distribution. It began the transition from terrestrial circuits to satellites in 1978, using Western Union's Westar satellites. In the early years of this system, it was functionally equivalent to cable TV distribution systems—a one-way, point-to-multipoint service to PBS affiliates throughout the country. The experience was favorable, and it set a useful precedent for the adoption of satellite program distribution by the major commercial networks.

2.4.2 The Major Commercial Broadcast Networks

When satellite program distribution service first became available, the commercial television networks were under no particular pressure to adopt it. They had worked with AT&T and its terrestrial system for many years, and the relationship was generally satisfactory. The extremely high value and the perishable nature of their program services made the networks reluctant to risk service interruptions with an unproven system.

Nevertheless, there were problems with the terrestrial system that made a change desirable. AT&T's video circuits did not reach all the affiliates and could not provide service to or from points that were far removed from its switching centers. The networks were concerned that AT&T had the monopoly power to raise its rates to unreasonable levels. Finally, there was the positive example of PBS. As a result, the major networks began serious study of the use of satellites in 1980.

At present, commercial networks' operational requirements are more complex than those of PBS in its early years. PBS was initially a one-way distribution system, while commercial networks have complex two-way systems. Program segments often originate in several different locations, and multiple program schedules are distributed to different groups of stations. Their satellite distribution systems, therefore, require intricate switching facilities.

In spite of these concerns and problems, the advantages of satellites were a sufficient motivation for the networks to begin large-scale use of satellites in 1984 after years of study.

NBC was the first of the major commercial TV networks to utilize satellites for program distribution. NBC began the transition in January 1984 and completed it a year later. After long study, it opted to use the Ku band in the continental United

States (CONUS), concluding that its higher power and freedom from terrestrial interference outweighed the problem of occasional rain outages.

The other networks quickly followed NBC into satellite distribution. They all use C-band transponders for distribution although some use Ku-band channels for electronic news gathering (ENG) (see Section 2.4.5).

2.4.3 Specialized and Ad Hoc Networks

The flexibility and relatively low cost of satellite distribution has led to the growth of specialized and *ad hoc* television networks. As with cable television, this development was accelerated by the deregulation of TVROs and their rapidly lowering costs. Most commercial TV stations now have TVROs and are able to receive satellite signals.

Specialized networks offer programming for regional and national affiliates that is not available on the major networks. The distribution of television pickups of the games of a professional sports team to a group of stations on a scheduled basis is an example of a specialized network service.

Ad hoc networks are formed to distribute a single event to a group of stations.

Specialized and ad hoc networks frequently do not own and operate their own distribution networks, and they often find it more economical to lease it from *resale carriers*. Resale carriers lease facilities on a wholesale basis from satellite and terrestrial carriers, integrate them as required for a specific application, and rent them to the networks. The function of resale carriers is described in Chapter 8.

2.4.4 Program Syndication

Program syndicators are entrepreneurs who obtain the rights to programs and sell individual stations the rights to broadcast them. Their best customers are independent (unaffiliated) stations, but many network affiliates broadcast syndicated programs as well.

The original method of distributing syndicated programs was to record them on tape and "bicycle" the tape from station to station. Each station made a copy before forwarding it to the next station. While this was an acceptable method, it was not conducive to the highest technical quality.

As the number of stations equipped with TVROs increased, it became practical to distribute syndicated programs by satellite. Stations then receive and record the programs. As compared with bicycling, satellite distribution is faster, better, and, in some cases, cheaper. It is now an accepted industry practice.

The technical facilities required for the distribution of syndicated programs is the same as those for specialized networks, except that the program material is usually recorded rather than live.

2.4.5 Electronic News Gathering

In some respects the use of satellites for electronic news gathering (ENG), or SNG for satellite news gathering, has had a more dramatic effect on the broadcasting industry than satellite distribution of network programs. Through the use of Ku-band earth stations, on-the-spot live coverage of news events has become practical in situations where C-band or microwave transmission are not possible. Most major television stations now have portable ENG earth station facilities for this purpose as well as to cover sporting events.

2.4.6 TV Broadcast Station Earth Station Facilities

A television broadcast station in a major metropolitan market typically has five or six earth stations. The complement might include primary and backup stations for receiving the network feed, a mobile SNG truck with Ku-band uplink and downlink facilities, a fixed Ku-band downlink station, and two or three C-band downlink stations for receiving syndicated programs and commercials.

2.5 DIRECT-TO-HOME BROADCASTING

The use of satellites for direct-to-home broadcasting was forecasted by industry pioneers in the earliest days of satellite communications. It was given the names *direct-to-home* (DTH) or *direct broadcast satellite* (DBS) service. It started in a totally unexpected way.

2.5.1 Backyard Dishes

It was originally believed that the power level permitted for C-band satellites was too low to be practical for home reception, and that direct-to-home service would require medium power Ku-band or high-power DBS satellites (see Chapter 3). To the surprise of the technical community, however, the public has been satisfied with the quality of C-band transmissions as received on the low-cost earth stations called backyard dishes. The pirating by the public of C-band programming intended for cable TV systems was so widespread that it became necessary to scramble the signals so that they could be received only by authorized earth stations.

2.5.2 The Direct-to-Home Broadcasting Market

Direct-to-home broadcasting in most cases must compete with cable. For a reasonable monthly fee, a cable TV system delivers to the home a multitude of programs, most of which the cable operator receives by satellite. In addition, cable systems usually provide local and regional broadcast signals. However, the number of channels on cable is limited and picture quality is not always the best. An opportunity was perceived to introduce DBS systems with more channels and higher-quality signals. Both are made possible by digital technology and can be offered at prices competitive with cable. A higher per-subscriber initial investment is required for DBS (the earth station) than for cable but many DBS entrepreneurs have partially subsumed this into their monthly fees. These features with reasonable cost have caused the DBS market to grow rapidly in the past two years. At the end of 1996, there were about 5 million DBS receivers installed.

DBS also applies to households that have no immediate prospects for the availability of cable TV. In the United States this is estimated to be about 15 million homes.

2.5.3 The Power-Antenna Size Trade-Off

The design of direct-to-home broadcast systems is dominated by the tradeoffs between satellite power, TVRO antenna size (and hence cost), and picture quality. For a level of picture quality judged to be satisfactory by the public, the tradeoff for typical systems is shown in Table 2.1.

A complete tradeoff comparison must include the cost of the satellite. This favors C band because the cost of C-band transponders, whether leased or purchased, is considerably lower.

2.5.4 C-Band Program Distribution

The larger size of C-band antennas did not prove to be a serious barrier to the sale of C-band backyard dishes. A trickle of installations began in 1980, and by 1982 it had become a flood. By 1987 the number of backyard dish installations was estimated to be nearly 2 million.

As the number of low-cost C-band backyard dishes proliferated, signal pirating became a serious problem to the suppliers of pay TV service and cable TV operators. The solution was to scramble the signals so that special descrambling equipment, at first available only to cable TV systems, was required to receive a useable picture.

When scrambling began in 1987, there was a precipitous drop in the sale of new backyard dishes. Sales recovered, at least partially, as descramblers were made available to the public; and at the end of 1989 it was estimated that more than 2.8 million backyard dishes were in use and that they were being added at the rate of 30,000 per month.[2] This growth has slowed as a result of Ku-band DBS availability.

2.5.5 Ku-Band Program Distribution

The Ku band seemed to present an even better opportunity than C band for cable TV program suppliers to broaden their market to include backyard dish owners in areas not served by cable. Because of the higher downlink power density at Ku band, the required backyard dish antenna diameter would only be half as great as for C band, and this was expected to increase the backyard dish audience. As with C band, the

Table 2.1 Tradeoff between Antenna Size and Transmitter Power

	Band		
	C	Ku	DBS
Transponder power (W)	4 to 10	45 to 60	150 to 250
Footprint coverage	CONUS	CONUS	1/2 CONUS
Antenna diameter (ft)	4 to 10	2 to 5	0.75 to 2.0

same downlink signal could serve both cable systems and backyard dishes, and distribution could be controlled by selective descrambling.

A number of attempts have been made to extend the C-band backyard dish concept to Ku-band, none have succeeded. This is probably because most homes who needed the service had already invested in C-band equipment. Now, this possibility has been overtaken by the digital DBS services (see Section 2.5.7).

2.5.6 Scrambling

Backyard-dish manufacturers and the more than 2 million owners mounted intense political opposition to the scrambling of satellite signals. It was even proposed that scrambling be forbidden by law, thus making signal piracy legal. The issue was resolved, in part by industry actions taken in response to government pressure, and in part by copyright legislation—the Satellite Home Viewers Act of 1988—which authorized all but broadcast network programs to be transmitted to home viewers.

The industry actions were directed toward making it possible for backyard dish owners to have access to scrambled signals at a reasonable cost. To accomplish this it was necessary to establish a technical center with the capability of authorizing descrambling on a selective basis and an administrative organization to receive orders, bill subscribers, and provide a list of subscribers to the technical center. There was a strong sentiment that the administrative organization should be a *third* party service, that is, that it be affiliated neither with program suppliers nor with cable TV operators.

General Instruments established the technical facility, the GI DBS Authorization Center in La Jolla, California, which transmits a code by satellite or telephone line to the transmission facilities of program suppliers. They then use the code to activate authorized descramblers.

The National Rural Telecommunications Co-op (NRTC) was the original administrative organization, and it has since been joined by a number of private companies that offer service packages.

With these facilities, it is now possible for backyard dish owners to receive scrambled satellite programs for approximately the same cost as cable TV subscribers.

Scrambling has not been totally successful in eliminating the piracy of satellite transmissions by unauthorized viewers. One set of industry figures[3] indicates that 1.1 million descramblers have been sold, but only about 500,000 viewers have subscribed to scrambled services. The presumption is that the other 600,000 have found ways to modify the descramblers to operate without authorization. The industry trade association, the *Satellite Broadcasting and Communications Association* (SBCA), has formed the *Anti-Piracy Task Force* (APTF) to investigate signal thefts by unauthorized modification of VideoCipher equipment, or other means.

Scrambling and descrambling equipment is described in Section 4.2.

2.5.7 Direct Broadcast by Satellites (DBS)

Authorization for Ku-band DBS was made in 1982 and several companies and groups planned services. However, all failed to get off the ground. For example, STC, a subsidiary of Comsat, ordered three DBS satellites in 1982—two to launch and one as a ground spare. After the satellites were completed, STC was unable to obtain partners or financing to launch the satellites and offer a program service, and the satellites were never launched.

The real breakthrough for DBS did not come until the development of digital technology, which allows up to five TV channels to be broadcast by each satellite transponder. Hughes Electronics Corporation's DIRECTV® service went on-air in 1994 and has signed up more than 2 million subscribers to date. Three satellites are in orbit for this service and a similar service marketed by Unites States Satellite Broadcasting Corp. (USSB), a subsidiary of Hubbard Broadcasting. DIRECTV provides 150 channels of TV and uses a low-cost 45-cm dish receiver that is manufactured by a number of consumer electronics companies.

As described in Chapter 1, applicants for DBS satellites are assigned channels, rather than complete orbital slots, because most satellites do not have sufficient capacity to provide primary power to all of the transponders that could operate in a single slot. Channels are usually assigned in pairs: one for eastern CONUS, and one for western CONUS plus Alaska and Hawaii.

The outstanding DBS channel assignments for the United States are listed in Table 2.2.

2.6 PRIVATE TELEVISION SYSTEMS

In addition to the major usage of satellites for the distribution of broadcast and cable television programs intended for the public, there is a small but growing application of satellites in corporate and other private television systems. Although either C band or Ku band can be used, Ku band is the most common because of its smaller antennas and the absence of potential interference from terrestrial microwave systems.

Table 2.2 DBS Channel Assignments for the United States

Permittee	Slot	Transponders	Services
Hughes	101°	27	DIRECTV, USSB
EchoStar	119°	21	Dish-TV
Tempo	119°	11	

2.6.1 B-MAC Transmission

Since private television systems are closed-circuit, users are not required to transmit or utilize one of the standard color TV broadcasting formats (NTSC, PAL, or SECAM). B-MAC (Multiple Analog Components) is an attractive alternative. The signal information in B-MAC is sent in three components, *luminance* (Y), and *color differences* (R-Y and B-Y), rather than luminance and a color subcarrier(s) as in NTSC, PAL, or SECAM. The subcarrier is at the upper end of the video spectrum where the noise is greatest in an FM system. Thus B-MAC makes it possible to obtain satisfactory results with a weaker downlink signal. The B-MAC format is also well adapted to scrambling (see Section 4.2.3.3).

A typical B-MAC earth station employs a 4.5 meter Ku-band antenna for both uplink and downlink.

2.6.2 Very Small Aperture Terminal (VSAT) Networks

For teleconferencing applications with limited requirements for the portrayal of motion and resolution, satisfactory results can be obtained with VSAT networks that transmit digital signals at a 56 or 64 kbs rate.[4] The digital signal is processed for bandwidth compression, and picture quality adequate for teleconferencing can be achieved in this narrow bandwidth.

VSAT systems usually operate in the Ku band with 1.8 meter antennas. They are intended primarily for data communications, but extending their application to teleconferencing increases their value to their users.

2.7 INTERNATIONAL TELEVISION SERVICE

Satellites are used to a limited extent within the United States for long-haul, for example, coast-to-coast, television circuits; but this usage is not extensive because they must compete with terrestrial circuits. The most important application of point-to-point satellite television service is for transoceanic circuits where terrestrial facilities are limited or nonexistent. (This may change as fiber optic circuits become available.) Satellites are particularly useful for news broadcasts where real-time transmission is critically important.

2.7.1 Intelsat and Comsat

Initially, all intercontinental television traffic to and from the United States was carried on *Intelsat* satellites and *Comsat* earth stations in the United States and government-owned earth stations in other countries.

Intelsat is an international consortium, established by treaty between 108 countries, which owns and operates an extensive system of satellites for international communications services. Its ownership is shared by the members of the consortium in proportion to their usage of its facilities. Its primary focus is voice and data traffic, but it handles television signals as well. It owns no ground facilities, except for the TT&C stations (see Chapter 1) that control its satellites.

Comsat is a private company established by statute as the United States's chosen instrument to provide ground facilities for access to Intelsat satellites.

Originally, the services of at least four carriers were required to send or receive an overseas signal through the Intelsat/Comsat system: a United States carrier to connect the United States source or terminus with a Comsat earth station, a Comsat earth station to access the Intelsat satellite, an Intelsat satellite, and a foreign carrier (in most countries owned by the host government) to access the satellite at the other end of the circuit.

2.7.2 Competing International Services

Comsat and Intelsat were established as monopolies, but there was strong pressure in the United States to allow independent private companies to offer international television transmission service. Comsat and Intelsat opposed these proposals vigorously, and a debate developed reminiscent of the deregulation/divestiture issue with AT&T.

In 1984 the Reagan administration ruled that independent international television systems were required "in the national interest," and independent companies were permitted to apply for satellites to carry international television traffic. To protect Intelsat's economic interests, the ruling imposed strict conditions on these systems, the most important of which were a prohibition against providing a public telephone service and a requirement for "consultation" with Intelsat before a system could be authorized. There are two independent satellite services that have been authorized: PanAmSat in South America and Orion Satellite Corp. in Europe.

In an equally important development, Comsat sold its earth stations to United States satellite carriers and now provides a booking and coordinating service for Intelsat service through these stations. In cooperation with United States carriers, Comsat established 18 international *gateways,* each a former Comsat earth station, or with a direct connection to one. The gateways provide the uplink/downlink interconnection with the Intelsat satellites.

Service through these gateways can be ordered from Comsat or from the carrier that provides the interconnection between the point of origination and the gateway facility.

In a further liberalization of its policies, Comsat now permits (but does not encourage) technically qualified earth stations owned by domestic carriers to access Intelsat satellites directly, thus bypassing the gateway facility. This service must be ordered and coordinated through Comsat by the domestic carrier.

2.8 SATELLITE USAGE BY RADIO

The impetus for the use of satellites by radio networks came from an increased demand for high-fidelity stereo transmission. AT&T's intercity audio circuits, although conditioned to provide more bandwidth than voice circuits, were not adequate for true high-fidelity service. Network stations faced increased high-fidelity competition from independent stations, which were programmed locally; and it was necessary for networks to match their sound quality.

The first radio networks to use satellites were the Mutual Broadcasting System, National Public Radio, AP Radio, and RKO Radio Network beginning in 1978 and 1979. These networks used analog transmission. NBC, CBS, and ABC did not begin the use of satellites until five years later in 1983 and 1984, using digital transmission to improve the quality further.

The digital system used for audio program transmission was first known as the Audio Digital Distribution Service (ADDS), and is now called the Digital Audio Transmission Service (DATS).

Satellite program distribution has become standard for radio networks, both national and regional, and over 70 networks now use it.

2.9 TRANSPONDERS USED FOR TELEVISION PROGRAM TRANSMISSION

The listing of television services available on satellite transponders is volatile and changes frequently.[5] A recent (1997) issue of *Satellite TV Week*, a newspaper distributed to backyard dish users, shows more than 300 C-band transponders and 80 Ku-band transponders devoted to television programs, sources, or news feeds.

The total usage of transponders by television program services, more than 380, makes the television industry the largest market for satellite transmission in the United States.

Notes

1   ENG, or electronic news gathering, is generally used to designate any system that employs TV cameras (rather than photographic) at the scene. The TV signal may be transmitted to the station by microwave, satellite, or tape. SNG, or satellite news gathering, designates an ENG system that employs satellites for transmission of the signal.

2   As reported by Satellite Broadcasting & Communications Association (SB CA), *Television Digest,* Vol 30, No. 2, January 8, 1990.

3   *Telecom Highlights International,* September 20, 1989, p. 18.

4   Inglis, A.F., *Electronic Communications Handbook,* Chapter 18, McGraw-Hill, New York, 1988.

5   The *Satellite Channel Chart,* published bimonthly by WESTAT Communications, PO Box 434, Pleasanton, CA 94566, lists the services carried on each transponder together with its polarization, the audio subcarrier frequencies, the audio subcarrier services, and the type of scrambling.

3

Communication Satellites

3.1 SATELLITE CLASSIFICATIONS

Satellites are classified by their usage and their technical characteristics.

3.1.1 Usage Classifications

The FCC defines three basic usage classifications for United States communication satellites: fixed service satellites (FSS), mobile satellite service (MSS), and broadcast satellite service (BSS).

- Fixed satellite service is a generic term that is applied to communication services that are neither mobile nor broadcast. The application of this term to satellites is an extension of its application to earlier communication mediums, for example, microwave. This classification includes most existing communication satellites.
- Mobile satellite service is an emerging service that supports communication between arbitrary points on the ground, where either or both terminals may change location at any time, even while communicating. This service is not covered in this book.
- The broadcast satellite service classification is a special category for direct broadcasting from satellite to homes. The BSS spectrum allocation and technical regulations were established in response to the economic necessity of using inexpensive earth stations with low sensitivity receivers and small low-gain antennas of limited directivity.

Each of the above services have their own frequency bands (see Section 3.1.2.1).

3.1.2 Technical Classifications

The most important technical classifications are frequency spectrum bands and service areas.

3.1.2.1 Frequency Spectrum Bands

Three bands in the frequency spectrum are currently used for radio and television satellite communications: C-band FSS, Ku-band FSS, and Ku-band DBS. The

Table 3.1 Communication Satellite Frequency Bands and Wavelengths

	Uplink	*Downlink*
C band, FSS	5.925-6.425 GHz	3.700-4.200 GHz
Ku band, FSS	14.0-14.5	11.7-12.2
Ku band BSS	17.3-17.8	12.2-12.7
The corresponding wavelengths are as follows:		
C band, FSS	5.06-4.67 cm	8.11-7.14 cm
Ku band, FSS	2.14-2.07	2.56-2.46
Ku band BSS	1.73-1.68	2.46-2.36

uplink and downlink frequencies allocated to these bands are shown in Table 3.1. In addition, new services are being planned for the Ka band, which is in the range from 18 to 31 GHz.

The characteristics of satellite services in these three frequency bands are quite different with respect to propagation effects, equipment performance, and FCC regulation. Accordingly, the band in which a satellite operates has a major effect on its performance.

3.1.2.2 Service Areas

Satellite service areas vary widely in size, ranging from a metropolitan area to most of a hemisphere. The size of the service area is determined by the width of the satellite antenna beam, which, in turn, depends on the size of the satellite antenna—the larger the antenna, the narrower the beam. One classification system defines four area sizes, or beam widths: *global, regional, national,* and *spot.*

- Global beams cover the entire area of the earth that is visible from the satellite. They are used by Intelsat for international communications.
- Regional beams usually cover a group of countries, for example, western Europe.
- National beams cover all or a significant portion of a single country. Most domestic United States satellites are in this category, although those that serve the continental United States as well as Alaska and Hawaii may have beam widths equal to those of regional systems.
- Spot beams cover a limited area, and are used principally for point-to-point voice and data communications. They have found only limited application in television service.

Satellites designed for international voice and data communication often have a variety of antenna beam widths. The INTELSAT 707 satellite, for example, has one global beam and four spot beams.

3.2 COMPARISON OF C-BAND AND KU-BAND SATELLITES

The most important differences between C-band and Ku-band FSS satellites for television applications are frequency sharing, antenna size, downlink power limitation, costs, and rainfall attenuation.

3.2.1 Frequency Sharing

C-band satellite uplinks and downlinks share frequency bands allocated to common carrier microwave systems. The design, location, and operation of C-band satellites and earth stations must be restricted to avoid interference to or from the other services that share the bands. Ku-band satellite systems have exclusive use of their allocated frequency band and, therefore, are not restricted by sharing considerations.

3.2.2 Antenna Size

Ku-band antennas are smaller for a given beam width because of the shorter wavelength.

3.2.3 Downlink Power Limitation

Because of the sharing situation discussed in Section 3.2.1, C-band satellites are limited to lower downlink power levels to avoid interference with terrestrial microwave systems. Ku-band satellites have no such limitation and can operate at higher power within the limitations of the power source of the satellite. This generally permits the use of smaller downlink antennas in the Ku band.

3.2.4 Earth Station Costs

In the past, C-band earth station costs were lower, in part because they were manufactured in greater volume than Ku-band earth stations. This has changed with the growth of DBS in the Ku band; DBS earth stations are less than one-third the cost of backyard C-band stations.

3.2.5 Satellite Costs

The cost of Ku-band transponders, either lease or sale, is substantially higher than C-band. Most Ku-band satellites have fewer transponders, and they are higher-powered. A typical monthly lease rate for a C-band transponder (preemptible) is $80,000 while, for a Ku-band transponder, it is $180,000. With digital modulation, it is possible to transmit two or more TV signals per transponder, which reduces the cost per channel.

3.2.6 Rainfall Attenuation

C-band transmissions suffer little if any attenuation when passing through regions of high rainfall. Ku-band signal transmissions, by contrast, are subject to degradation from heavy rainfall, particularly in tropical and subtropical areas where cloudbursts occur frequently. Ku-band rainfall attenuation of 6 to 10 dB or more occurs during heavy rain and, if reliable transmission is required under such conditions, the link design (see Section 5.3) must provide a suitable margin.

3.2.7 Current C- and Ku-Band Usage

As the result of its lower cost and freedom from rainfall attenuation, together with its advantage of being first in the marketplace, C-band service is more commonly used for television communications services other than DBS. The Ku band, however, is almost universally used for portable SNG service (see Section 2.1) because of its smaller antennas and freedom from interference to and from microwave systems, which removes any limitations on where an earth sattion may be set up. NBC uses the Ku band as the primary distribution medium for service to its affiliates. With the growth of DBS, the total number of Ku-band earth stations will soon exceed the number of C-band earth stations.

3.3 COMMUNICATION SATELLITE DESIGN

The two primary systems of a communication satellite are the *bus* and the *payload*.[1]

3.3.1 The Satellite Bus

The satellite bus consists of a housing structure and three major operating subsystems:

1. the power system, which provides a continuous source of primary power for both the bus and the payload;
2. a command and control system, which monitors the operating condition of the satellite and executes operational commands from the TT&C (tracking, telemetry, and command) earth station; and
3. a station keeping system for maintaining the satellite in the proper position and attitude in its orbital slot.

3.3.1.1 Satellite Housing Structures

The configuration of the satellite housing is determined by the system employed to stabilize the position and attitude of the satellite in its orbital slot (station keeping).

Three-axis-stabilized satellites employ internal *momentum wheels*, which rotated at 4,000 to 6,000 RPM in early satellites. This required constant energy to keep the wheels rotating. The modern approach uses momentum wheels that rotate only when attitude changes are required—this is called *zero momentum* stabilization.

The housing of a three-axis satellite is rectangular with external features, as shown in Figure 3.1. The solar cells are mounted on flat panels that rotate once each day about an axis parallel to the earth's axis so that they always face the sun. During launch, the solar panels and antennas are folded against the housing. They are deployed after the satellite reaches its geosynchronous orbit.

An alternative design uses *spin stabilization.* The housing of a spin-stabilized satellite is cylindrical and rotates around its axis slightly more than once each second to provide the gyroscopic effect. The antenna must remain pointed in a fixed direction as the satellite spins; and it is *despun,* that is, connected to the body of the satellite by a rotating bearing.

In spin-stabilized satellites, the solar cells are mounted on the cylindrical surface of the satellite. Since only a fraction of the cells are facing the sun at any given time, a larger number of cells must be used. This limits the power capability and, thus, the range of application of these satellites.

3.3.1.2 Power System

Satellites operate all their electrical systems from solar power generated by arrays of *solar cells* that convert radiant energy from the sun into electrical energy. On-board storage batteries are used to provide a continuous source of power through an eclipse period. These are usually nickel-cadmium or nickel-hydrogen to provide maximum life and reliability.

The power requirements of the satellites used for DBS are so great that it is not always practical to provide sufficient battery capacity to maintain power, even for the brief periods of solar eclipses. The effect of signal interruptions in this service can be mitigated by locating the satellite to the west of the desired service area, thus causing the eclipses to occur after midnight.

3.3.1.3 Command and Control System

The command and control system includes instrumentation for monitoring all the vital operating parameters of the satellite, telemetry circuits for relaying this information to the TT&C earth station, a subsystem for receiving and interpreting commands sent to the satellite from the TT&C, and a command subsystem for controlling the operation of the satellite.

3.3.1.4 Station Keeping

Although gravity and centrifugal forces are nominally in balance on the satellite, there are minor disturbing forces or perturbations that would cause the satellite to drift out of its slot if uncompensated. The gravitational effect of the sun and moon are examples. Another is the South American land mass which tends to pull satellites southward.

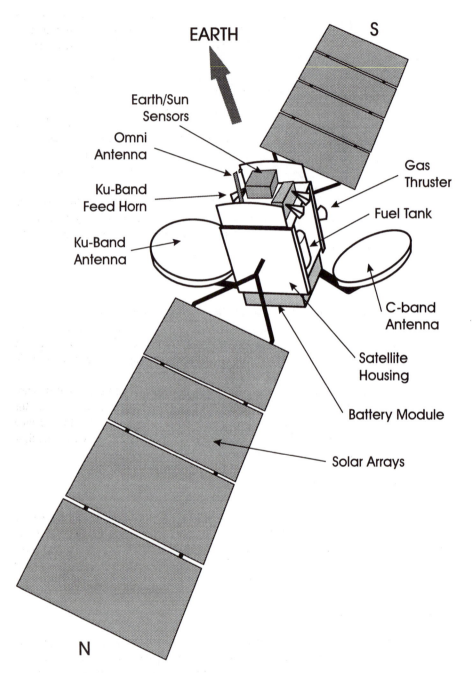

Figure 3.1 A three-axis-stabilized satellite.

The physical mechanism for maintaining the satellite in its slot, *station keeping,* is the controlled ejection of gas from thruster nozzles, which protrude through the satellite's case. The momentum of the gas stream produces an equal and opposite change in momentum of the satellite, which restores the satellite to its proper position. Hydrazine gas is used for this purpose, and at the beginning of the satellite's life several hundred pounds of it are stored in the propellant tanks. It is emitted from the thrusters as required to maintain the satellite in its slot. The supply is eventually exhausted, typically after 10 years, and this usually ends the useful life of the satellite.

Sensors are used on the satellite to monitor the positions of earth and sun as seen from the satellite. These assist in the station keeping process. An omnidirectional antenna is also used to support communication regardless of the satellite's attitude; this is necessary in the initial acquisition of the satellite and also if an incident causes loss of attitude control.

3.3.1.5 Beacons

Each satellite has two or more beacon transmitters—one for each polarization—operating at the ends of its 500 MHz spectrum, others for redundancy. The beacon antennas are located to not interfere with the payload antennas and they perform important roles in the operation of the system. The beacon transmitters send telemetry and ranging signals and also provide an aiming point for locating the satellite during the installation of a new earth station. They also provide the basis for automatic power level control for Ku-band uplinks. The strength of their signals is monitored; and if it is attenuated by rainfall, the uplink power can be increased to compensate.

3.3.2 The Satellite Payload

Satellites exist in order to carry their payloads. The payload of a communications satellite has four major subsystems:

- the receiving antennas,
- the receivers,
- the transponders, and
- the transmitting antennas.

These are combined in a variety of configurations in accordance with the satellite's design objectives.

3.3.2.1 Frequency Reuse

The configuration of the payload is determined by the principle of frequency reuse, which is used on all geosynchronous satellites. Frequencies are used twice in the same satellite by cross-polarization of the radiated signals so that two transmission channels can occupy the same spectrum space. (Antennas designed for one kind of

Figure 3.2 C-band channel configuration.

polarization reject signals of the opposite polarization.) FSS communication satellites employ vertical and horizontal polarization on alternate channels, while BSS satellites employ right- and left-handed circular polarization. Figure 3.2 shows a typical configuration of C-band satellite channels with cross-polarization. Notice that the channel center frequencies of one polarization are interleaved between the channels of the other polarization. This further reduces signal crosstalk.

3.3.2.2 Payload Signal Path

The uplink signals pass from the satellite receiving antennas to the satellite receivers, each of which is tuned to a group of channels of a single polarization. The outputs of the receivers are downconverted by a mixer and local oscillator in the receiver. These signals feed arrays of transponders, which contain one HPA per channel to amplify the signals for transmission back to earth. The transponders are the heart of the active satellite payload, and their power and bandwidth establish the most significant specifications of the satellite.

The number of transponders on a satellite can be limited either by the availability of spectrum space or by the available primary power. Spectrum space limits the capacity of most communication satellites, which are designed so that their carriers completely occupy the frequency bands allocated for that class of satellite. However, the availability of primary power may limit the number of channels on a DBS satellite. Because of this, some DBS systems use several satellites located in the same orbital slot in order to use all the available channels. Since the satellites are so close together, the users can set their antenna to a single position that will receive all the signals.

3.3.2.3 Satellite Antennas

Satellite antennas are usually parabolic reflectors with feed horns located near their focal points. This format is very flexible, and many variations in design parameters are possible. Among these are the polarization of the radiated signal, the gain and directivity of the antenna, and the beam's shape and direction. The beam shape and antenna gain are determined primarily by the size and shape of the reflector—the larger the reflector, the narrower the beam and the higher the gain. Complex beam shapes are achieved with either feed horn arrays or shaping of the reflector surface. The direction of the beam can be controlled within limits by the location of the feed horn with respect to the axis of the parabola.

Since satellites are usually designed to provide communication service to a relatively large area, the antenna beams must be broad, and the antenna gains comparatively low. The low antenna gain does not present a difficulty in the uplink where the satellite receives a strong signal from a high-power transmitter at the uplink earth station. It is a problem for the downlink, particularly in point-to-multipoint service where the cost of earth stations can be critical. Downlink design, therefore, often involves a number of significant trade-offs.

3.3.2.4 Satellite Receivers

Since communication satellites normally receive strong uplink signals, the performance of their receivers is less critical than that of the earth station receivers.

3.3.2.5 Satellite Transponders

The choice of transponder bandwidth and power are fundamental in the design of satellites.

For C-band satellites there is a *defacto* channel-spacing standard of 40 MHz. The active channel bandwidth is 36 MHz, which leaves 4 MHz for guard bands between channels. Ku band does not have the same degree of standardization, and channel bandwidths range from 24 to 72 MHz.

The choice of power is more complex. Higher-power transponders are more costly, and this creates an economic trade-off between satellite and earth station costs. C-band downlink power is rather severely limited by FCC Rules. Finally, there are technical limits to the maximum power capability of satellite transponders.

Typical power ratings of satellite transponders currently in use (1997) are as follows:

Satellite type	Power (W)
C-band, FSS	12 to 20
Ku-band, FSS	20 to 110
Ku-band, BSS	120 to 200

Early satellites used *travelling wave tubes* (TWTs) for the transponder power amplifiers. Developments in solid state technology have made it possible to use high-efficiency *solid-state power amplifiers* (SSPAs) in many C-band satellites. SSPAs are both more linear and more reliable than TWTs. TWTs are still used in high-power DBS satellites.

All transponder power amplifiers share a common characteristic known as *saturation*. This is the power level at which an increase in input power results in no further increase in the output power; in fact, it may decrease slightly. Operating close to the saturation point, then, produces the maximum power output for the transponder.

In cases where there is more than one carrier per transponder, operation must be somewhat below saturation to avoid intermodulation distortion that would cause interference between the carriers.

For the satellite user, the most important measure of a satellite's power is its *effective isotropic radiated power (EIRP)*. This is the ratio (in decibels) between the strength of its downlink signal at a given point on the earth to the strength of a signal from an *isotropic radiator* that is radiating one watt from the orbital slot. (An isotropic radiator is an imaginary antenna that radiates equally in all directions. It cannot be physically constructed.[2]) Satellite operators publish EIRP contour maps of their satellites, and their use in system design is described in Chapter 5.

3.3.2.6 Transponder Traffic Capacity

The traffic capacity of a transponder is determined by its power and bandwidth.

C-band transponders are normally used for one television channel including video, audio, and possibly one or more narrow band communication or data channels. With their greater bandwidth and power, Ku-band transponders are frequently used to transmit two television channels or, with digital modulation, up to five television channels for each 24 MHz transponder (see Section 5.4.1.5).

3.4 C-BAND FSS SATELLITES

3.4.1 Channel Configuration

Each C-band communications satellite is allocated 500 MHz of spectrum space. Frequency reuse by cross-polarization is required by FCC rules; and it is universal practice (see Section 3.3.2.1) to divide the satellite spectrum into 24 channels—each 36 MHz wide with 4 MHz guard bands, for a total of 40 MHz. This channel width follows a precedent set by microwave systems, which operate in the same region of the spectrum.

The channel configuration on a dual-polarized C-band communications satellite was shown in Figure 3.2. The center frequencies of alternate channels are spaced by one-half the channel width so that the unmodulated carrier and most of the energy of a modulated carrier falls in the guard band of the adjacent channels. Staggering the channel center frequencies, together with the isolation provided by cross-polarization, reduces the crosstalk between adjacent channels to a negligible level for television transmission systems.

3.4.2 Downlink Power Density

The *downlink power density* is the radiated power per unit area and per kHz of bandwidth. It is limited for C-band satellites by international agreement in order to minimize interference with terrestrial microwave systems.[3]

The downlink power density of a carrier that is frequency-modulated with a television signal and employing energy dispersal (see Section 4.2.1.3) is limited to an EIRP of about 38 dBW at low elevation angles to 48 dBW for elevation angles above 25°. The maximum EIRP of a typical C-band footprint is typically 34 to 38 dBW.

3.5 KU-BAND FSS SATELLITES

3.5.1 Channel Configuration

As with C band, most Ku-band satellites employ cross-polarized feeds on alternate channels to double the spectrum capacity. The channel configuration is similar to that shown in Figure 3.2. Unlike C-band, however, there is no standard industry practice for channel bandwidth and this varies from 24 to 72 MHz in different satellites. This lack of standardization makes it difficult to use cross-polarization as a technique for reducing interference between adjacent satellites (see Section 5.5.4).

Increasing the channel bandwidth increases the individual transponder power because the total power of the satellite power source is divided among a smaller number of transponders. It also makes possible a greater frequency deviation of an FM signal. The higher transponder power and greater frequency deviation both lead to a reduced requirement for the downlink antenna size. This advantage is offset to some extent, particularly in the high rain areas of the Gulf coast, by the need for a greater *fade margin* for the Ku band (see Section 5.3.2). In the case of digital modulation, designers have additional parameters that enter the tradeoff between bandwidth and power (see Section 4.2.2).

The most widely used configuration for Ku-band satellites now is 24 cross-polarized channels, each with a 36 MHz bandwidth.

3.5.2 Downlink Power Density Limitations

Since Ku-band satellites do not share frequencies with terrestrial services, there is no FCC limitation on downlink power density.

3.6 HYBRID FSS SATELLITES

Hybrid satellites have both C-band and Ku-band transponders.

3.6.1 Description

As the power capability of satellite designs has increased, the hybrid satellite concept has become more popular. Table 1.1 lists hybrid satellites now operational. They have a variety of configurations, but the FCC requires that new hybrids fully utilize the 500 MHz bandwidth of each band.

3.6.2 Applications

In addition to their greater capacity, which leads to a lower price per transponder, hybrid satellites have the obvious advantage of providing the user a choice of frequency bands. They pose the further possibility of using different bands for the uplink and downlink portions of a signal path. This is accomplished in the satellite by a technique known as *cross-strapping* but at this time, it is only used in some AT&T satellites. Both CBS and ABC use Ku band for SNG uplinks and C band for downlinks on hybrid satellites.

3.7 BSS SATELLITES

3.7.1 International System Specifications

BSS system specifications have been established by international agreement, most recently by a meeting of the World Administrative Radio Conference (WARC) in 1979; and, for the western hemisphere, by a meeting of the Regional Administrative Radio Conference (RARC) in 1983. The purpose of the specifications was to make it possible for members of the public to enjoy satisfactory reception with small receiving antennas (approximately 1 foot in diameter) and low-priced receivers. To achieve this objective the agreement contained the following provisions:

1. BSS was allocated a portion of the K band. This avoided the problem of interference with terrestrial microwave systems and made a higher downlink EIRP possible.
2. The maximum permitted EIRP was 56 dBW at the edge of the coverage area It was recommended that the EIRP at the center of the coverage area be 3 dB higher than at the edge. This signal level would make it possible to achieve acceptable picture quality with an inexpensive receiver and an antenna as small as 1 foot in diameter.
3. Right- and left-handed circular polarization would be used to achieve frequency reuse. Each polarization would have sixteen 24 or 27 MHz channels.
4. The spacing between orbital slots would be 9° rather than 2° as with the Ku band and C band. This is necessary because the effective beam width of a one-foot antenna in the BSS band is about 8°.

Table 3.2 Typical BSS Satellite Specifications

Country	U.S.	Japan	Europe
Operator	DIRECTV	NHK	Eutelsat
Satellite designation	DBS-1	BS-3N	Hot Bird-1
Signal modulation	Digital	Digital	D2-MAC
Number of transponders	16	3	16
Transponder bandwidth (MHz)	24	27	36
Frequency reuse	No	No	No
Polarization	Circular	Circular	Linear
Transponder power	120 W	120 W	70 W
Coverage	CONUS	Honshu	Europe
EIRP (edge of coverage)	48 dBW	56 dBW	44 dBW
Receiving antenna diameter	45 cm		

3.7.2 BSS Satellite Specifications

The specifications of three of the BSS satellites that have been built to date are shown in Table 3.2.

Notes

1 The Hughes Space and Communications World Wide Web site has a lot of information about satellites: http://www.hughespace.com.

2 The use of an isotropic radiator as the reference antenna for satellite systems differs from the practice in television broadcasting where the half-wave dipole is commonly used. An isotropic radiator cannot be physically constructed, but theoretical calculations are more convenient.

3 The power limitation within any 4 kHz band is -152 dBW/m^2 for elevation angles below 5°, $[-152 + (0°-5°)/2]$ dBW/m^2 for elevation angles, 0°, between 5° and 25° and -142 dBW/m^2 for elevation angles above 25°, See Appendix A.1 for conversion to EIRP.

4

Earth Stations

This chapter describes the functions and performance specifications of the principal components of the satellite earth stations used for the transmission and distribution of radio and television programs.

4.1 ANTENNAS

4.1.1 Antenna Types

Earth station antennas must be highly directional. In the transmit mode, they radiate energy in a narrow beam; and in the receive mode, they extract the radiant energy that arrives within the angular boundaries of this beam. The antenna's directivity is responsible for its gain, both transmitting and receiving, and makes it possible for adjacent satellites, separated by only 2° (9° for DBS satellites) on the orbital arc, to operate on the same frequencies.

Most satellite earth station antennas consist of a reflector and one or more feed horns, which illuminate the reflector with radiant energy in the transmit mode and collect it from the reflector in the receive mode.

Cross-polarized feed horns with a separate feed for each polarization are used for transmitting or receiving antennas in systems that operate with two polarizations.

Antennas with one feed horn system have a single beam, while multiple feed horns can be used to produce multiple beams.

Since uplinks and downlinks operate on different frequencies, the same antenna can be used simultaneously for transmission and reception. This requires a waveguide filter in the coupling network to prevent leakage of transmitter power into the receiver.

4.1.1.1 Single-Beam Antennas

In the most basic single-beam-antenna configuration, the reflector is a section of a paraboloid; and the feed horn, located at its focus, illuminates it directly. This is known as a *prime-focus-feed* antenna, shown in Figure 4.1(a).

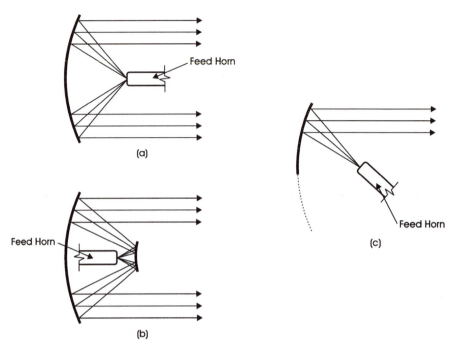

Figure 4.1 (a) Prime-focus-feed antenna, (b) Dual-reflector antenna, (c) Offset-feed antenna.

The dual-reflector antenna [Figure 4.1(b)] is an important variation. The feed horn is aimed away from the main reflector; its beam is intercepted by a subreflector and reflected back to the main reflector.

Dual-reflector antennas come in a variety of configurations, depending on the shape of the two reflectors. If the subreflector is convex toward the main reflector as in Figure 4.1, it is known as a *Cassegrain* antenna. If it is concave, it is known as a *Gregorian.* In still another variation known as the *Gregux,* the subreflector consists of a concave ring.

A third variation, the *offset-feed* antenna shown in Figure 4.1(c), is based on the prime-focus-feed type where the dish is an of-center section of a paraboloid. It has the advantage that the feed horn and its support are not in the way of the signal beam. This design is adaptable to low costs and it is widely used for DBS receivers.

Antenna designs are the result of a complex series of trade-offs between cost, directivity, and gain. Prime-focus-fed antennas are more inexpensive, suffer less loss of radiant energy by blockage, and, for lower gain antennas, have lower-level *sidelobes.* Dual-reflector antennas have greater design flexibility and offer a greater choice of trade-offs. The three most common configurations used in satellite systems are the prime-focus-feed, the Cassegrain, and the offset-feed. C-band receive-only stations frequently employ prime-focus feeds, while higher gain Cassegrain antennas are often used for C-band transmit-receive systems and for the Ku band.

4.1.1.2 Multiple-Beam Antennas

If the feed horn is located on the axis of the main reflector, the antenna beam will be directed along this axis, but the beam can be pointed in other directions by offsetting the feed horn from the axis. Offset feeding degrades the performance of antennas somewhat, but it has almost become the standard for DBS receiving antennas. Offset-feeding's other main application is in multiple-beam antennas.

Multiple-beam antennas are used in downlink earth stations that receive signals from several satellites, for example, at cable TV head-ends. They offer considerable economy, and occupy less space as compared with the use of a separate antenna for each satellite.

Multibeam antennas offer a considerable challenge to designers, and a variety of configurations has been developed. One uses a spherical rather than a paraboloidal reflector; another uses a combination spherical and paraboloidal surface and is called a *torus*.

In the simplest spherical configuration, feed horns are placed along the focal surface of the spherical reflector and directed toward its interior surface. The direction of each beam is coincident with the axis of its feed. This configuration has the advantage that antenna beams can be directed over a wide range of angles.

The shape of the torus antenna reflector is more complex. The surface is circular in the plane of the feeds, but parabolic in the orthogonal (right angle) plane. The use of a parabolic surface in one plane results in superior performance in some configurations as compared with the spherical antenna.

4.1.2 Electrical Performance Criteria

The most important electrical performance criteria of transmitting and receiving antennas are directivity, gain, and polarization isolation. They are reciprocal for the transmitting and receiving modes, and the same specifications apply to both. For receiving antennas, the *noise temperature* is also important, although in practice it is determined more by the elevation angle of the beam than by the antenna design. (See the definition of noise temperature in Section 4.4.2. and see Chapter 5 for its effect on the performance of a satellite system.)

4.1.2.1 Antenna Directivity

The radiation pattern of earth station antennas consists of a very narrow main beam surrounded by side lobes of much smaller amplitude (see Figure 4.2). The directivity of these antennas, that is, the extent to which they concentrate the radiated or received energy in a single direction, is important for two reasons:

1. It determines the effectiveness of the antenna in discriminating against signals from adjacent satellites when receiving, and in avoiding interference to these satellites when transmitting; and
2. It is the most important factor in determining the antenna's gain.

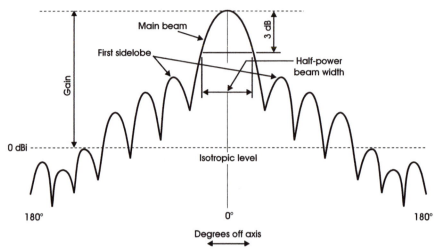

Figure 4.2 Earth station antenna radiation pattern.

An antenna's directivity is completely specified by its radiation pattern. For many purposes, however, it is sufficient to specify two parameters, the *half-power beam width (HPBW),* and the *first sidelobe amplitude.*

The HPBW is the angle between the points on the radiation pattern at which the radiated power density is one-half its density at maximum. As a first approximation, the HPBW is proportional to the ratio of the wavelength to the diameter of the antenna reflector, or, for a noncircular reflector, to its dimension in the plane in which the beam width is specified. A trade-off can be made between beam width and sidelobe amplitude by controlling the uniformity of reflector illumination. Uniform reflector illumination gives the narrowest beam width, but also results in the largest sidelobes—only 15 dB below the main lobe. A typical trade-off between beam width and sidelobes occurs with edge illumination 13 dB below the center. The side lobe level is 23 dB below the main lobe for this design. By illuminating the center more strongly than the edges, the sidelobe amplitude is reduced, but at the expense of gain and HPBW. The trade-off between beam width and sidelobe amplitude is basic in antenna design.

Table 4.1 shows the HPBW and the beam width between nulls of typical C- and Ku-band antennas. The trade-off between HPBW and sidelobe amplitude in the antennas in these examples results in a first sidelobe that is 23 dB below the main beam. See Appendix A.2 for the equations for calculating antenna beam widths.

4.1.2.2 FCC Directivity Specifications

The FCC has established specifications for the directivity of uplink antennas in order to minimize interference to adjacent satellites with 2° spacing. There are no mandatory requirements for downlink antennas, but the same standards are recom-

Table 4.1 Typical Antenna Specifications

	Antenna diameter (meters)	HPBW (degrees)	Null BW (degrees)	Gain (dBi)*
C-band downlink				
(4 GHz, 7.5 cm wavelength)				
	2	2.6	6.4	36.6
	5	1.05	2.5	44.5
	7	0.75	1.8	47.4
	10	0.52	1.3	50.6
C-band uplink				
(6 GHz, 5.0 cm wavelength)				
	5	0.70	1.7	48.0
	7	0.50	1.2	50.9
	10	0.35	0.85	54.0
Ku-band downlink				
(12 GHz, 2.5 cm wavelength)				
	1	1.75	4.2	40.0
	2	0.88	2.1	46.0
	5	0.35	0.95	54.0
	7	0.25	0.60	56.9
Ku-band uplink				
(14 GHz, 2.14 cm wavelength)				
	2	0.75	1.8	47.4
	5	030	0.72	55.3
	7	0.21	0.51	58.4

* Decibels above the energy density from an isotropic radiator radiating the same power.

mended. The protection to licensed downlink stations from co-channel stations is based on the assumption that these standards are met. Table 4.2 lists the maximum permissible gain envelope relative to an isotropic radiator in the angular range from 1° to 7° off the main beam and in the plane of the geosynchronous orbit.

Since the first null of most uplink antennas is less than 1° from the axis of the main beam (see Table 4.1), it is the sidelobes rather than the main beam which must be controlled to meet this specification.

4.1.2.3 Antenna Gain

The gain of a transmitting antenna is the ratio, usually expressed in decibels, between the power density radiated at the peak of its beam to the power density from an isotropic radiator (see Section 3.3.2.5).

Table 4.2 Maximum Off-Axis Gain Permitted by FCC Rules (Plane of Orbital Arc)

Off-Beam angle (degrees)	Maximum gain (dBi)
1	29.0
2	21.5
3	17.0
4	14.0
5	11.6
6	9.6
7	8.0

Source: *FCC Rules and Regulations Satellite Communications,* Title 47, Part 25, Sec. 25.209 of the Code of Federal Regulations. Washington, D.C.: Government Printing Office.

The HPBW is the primary factor determining the antenna gain—the narrower the beam width, the greater the concentration of radiated power and the higher the gain.

The gain is also influenced by the antenna efficiency—the fraction of the power emitted by the feed horn that is radiated in the main beam. The antenna efficiency is determined by a variety of factors, such as power spillover at the edges of reflectors, power blocked by the feed horn and subreflector, power absorbed by reflector surfaces, and power lost in the sidelobes. The efficiency of practical satellite antenna designs varies from 50 to 85 percent.

The equation for calculating antenna gain is given in Appendix A.3. Other factors being equal, it is approximately proportional to the ratio of the area of the reflector to the square of the wavelength. The gains of representative satellite antennas, assuming efficiencies of 70 percent, are shown in Table 4.1.

Antenna performance is reciprocal for transmitting and receiving, but the gain is not the same in the receive mode as while transmitting because of the difference in uplink and downlink frequencies. Moreover, an antenna's effectiveness in extracting energy from a radio wave is determined not only by its gain but also by the wavelength of the radiation, since the received energy is proportional to the square of the wavelength. Thus a 2-meter antenna has a gain of 36.6 dBi at C band and 46.0 dBi at Ku band, but the higher Ku-band gain is offset by its shorter wavelength (one-third that of C band) and the received energy for the same EIRP is approximately the same. This suggests that antenna *area* rather than gain is the best indicator of its comparative effectiveness for receiving radiant energy at different wavelengths. Gain, however, is important for mathematical analysis and for comparisons at the same wavelength.

4.1.2.4 Polarization Isolation

Most satellites employ frequency reuse with differently polarized channels sharing the same frequencies (see Section 3.3.2.1). It is important that the antenna produce a high degree of isolation between cross-polarized channels, both for receiving and transmitting, to avoid mutual interference. See Chapter 6 for polarization isolation required by the FCC for uplinks. Satellite carriers typically require at least 30 dB for the uplinks to their satellites. This means that the strength of the cross-polarized components of uplink radiation must be at least 30 dB below the desired components.

4.1.3 Structural and Environmental Requirements

The antenna is the most exposed component of an earth station, and it is the most vulnerable to degraded performance or even destruction by adverse environmental conditions. These include wind, humidity, precipitation, icing, and the effects of salt atmosphere.

4.1.3.1 Mechanical Stability

A high degree of mechanical stability is a basic requirement of the antenna mounting structure. It must be capable of maintaining an acceptable stability even in the presence of icing and high winds. Wind loading of the antenna can cause pointing errors; and with beams less than one degree wide, a small error can cause a serious loss of signal. Unfortunately, as the diameter of the antenna and its wind loading increases, the amount of pointing error that can be tolerated must be reduced. Larger antennas require an extreme degree of rigidity to minimize pointing errors in high winds.

Two specifications are normally stated for antenna stability, *pointing accuracy* and *survival.* The pointing accuracy is defined in terms of the rms angular deflection (averaged over time) at stated levels of steady wind velocity and gusts. An example is 0.08° rms deflection with wind velocity of 45 mph gusting to 60 mph.

Survival is defined in terms of the wind velocity that can be tolerated from any direction without destruction or permanent damage to the antenna. An example is 100 mph without icing and 70 mph with 2 inches of radial ice.

The pointing accuracy of an antenna system is determined not only by the antenna structure but also by the stability of the base to which the antenna is mounted. The design of the base should take this into account, both with respect to short-term and long-term instabilities.

The specification for pointing accuracy is determined by the degree of reliability desired. Backyard-dish antennas with relatively low requirement for reliability but with a requirement for low cost can tolerate poorer pointing accuracy than antennas used in commercial service. Antennas used in uplinks must always have high pointing accuracy.

4.1.3.2 Other Environmental Factors

Humidity, especially in a salt atmosphere, can cause corrosion of electrical and mechanical components.

Precipitation brings with it the risk of leakage into sensitive electrical and electronic components.

Snow and ice forming on the antenna reflector can cause a serious degradation or even loss of signal. Deicers (see Section 4.1.4.4) are needed to protect the antenna in climates subject to snow and icing if reliable performance is required.

Table 4.3 lists typical environmental specifications for commercial earth stations with high reliability requirements.

4.1.4 Antenna Accessories

4.1.4.1 Antenna Pointing Facilities

It is essential that the antenna mounting structure be provided with facilities for pointing the antenna toward the desired satellite. They may be pointed manually or by motorized remote control.

With manual pointing, the elevation and azimuth are adjusted independently, sometimes known as *elevation-over-azimuth.*

With motorized control, a *polar mount* is often used. The antenna is mounted so that it can be rotated around an axis which is parallel to the earth's axis. After the antenna is initially aligned so that its beam is pointed toward a slot on the geosynchionous orbit, it will follow the orbit quite closely over a wide range of azimuths as it is rotated around the polar axis. The visible satellites can then be accessed with no manual adjustment of the antenna.

Table 4.3 Typical Antenna Environmental Specifications

Parameter	Specification
Ambient temperature	–20°C to +55°C
Wind loading (survival)	125 mph w.o. ice; 85 mph w. 2 in ice
Pointing error (60 mph wind)	
C band: (backyard 2m antenna)	0.5°
Ku band: (7m antenna)	0.05°
Precipitation	1 in/hr rain, or 0.25 in/hr freezing rain, or 1 in/hr snowfall
Relative humidity	0 to 10%
Static ice load	0.25 in radial ice or 4 in snowfall

4.1.4.2 Preset Positions

If the antenna must be moved from satellite to satellite frequently, a series of preset positions in the pointing mechanism is an extremely useful feature.

4.1.4.3 Polarization Control

The feed horn of the antenna must be adjusted so that it is aligned with the polarization of the satellite. This can be accomplished manually by rotating the feed horn at the antenna or remotely by a *ferrite polarizer*. The ferrite polarizer makes use of the *Faraday effect*, the rotation of the plane of polarization of an electromagnetic wave in the presence of a strong magnetic field.

4.1.4.4 Deicers

Deicing can be accomplished by means of electrical heating elements or by means of radomes. Electrical deicing may not be adequate in severe climates, and a radome around the reflector with a space heater to maintain its interior above freezing may be required.

4.2 SIGNAL PROCESSING

Much of the electronic complexity of an earth station is involved in the processing of audio and video signals for transmission and reception. The functions of the signal processing depend on the modulation method used (see Section 1.1.4). The most widely used methods in satellite communication are frequency modulation (FM) or digital modulation.

4.2.1 Frequency Modulation

FM is the preferred method of modulation for analog transmission over satellites. The input to the signal processor is analog video and audio and the output is one or more carriers modulated at an intermediate frequency, usually in the range of 70 to 140 MHz.

4.2.1.1 Video Preemphasis

It is an inherent characteristic of frequency modulation that the thermal noise in the output baseband spectrum increases linearly with frequency. This creates a special problem with NTSC and PAL waveforms because the color subcarrier frequency is in the high-noise region near the top of the baseband. In the absence of corrective measures, the signal-to-noise ratio of the chroma information in the picture would be unsatisfactory. This characteristic also creates a potential problem for the audio circuits although possibly not as severe.

The standard corrective technique is to *preemphasize* the high-frequency components of the baseband signals at the uplink transmitter and to provide *complementary deemphasis* at the downlink receiver. Preemphasis is required by the FCC for FM broadcasting and has become a standard technique for satellite transmissions. It produces a major improvement in the signal-to-noise ratio of both audio and video signals.

Since the receiver deemphasis characteristic must be complementary to the preemphasis, an industry standard is required. A commonly followed standard for video is ITU-R Recommendation F.405-1. This specifies approximately 13 dB of preemphasis at 4 MHz as compared with low frequencies (see Table 4.4). This preemphasis characteristic improves the video signal-to-noise ratio by approximately 11 dB; this is sometimes called the *deemphasis factor*.

4.2.1.2 Audio Preemphasis

The audio preemphasis standard is the same as for FM broadcasting—the response of an R-L circuit in which the time constant $\frac{L}{R}$ is 75 microseconds.

4.2.1.3 Sideband Energy Dispersal (C-Band)

Most of the energy in the spectrum of an RF carrier frequency modulated by a video signal is concentrated in sidebands in the immediate vicinity of the carrier. This creates a problem for C-band satellite systems because the FCC limits on downlink EIRP are based on the energy density per kHz of spectrum space.

The problem is overcome by adding a low-frequency energy dispersal signal to the video baseband signal before it modulates the carrier. This spreads the sideband energy over a larger region of the spectrum, reducing the energy density per kHz in the downlink signal and increasing the permissible EIRP.

Table 4.4 Video Preemphasis Characteristic—ITU-R Rec. F.405-1

Baseband frequency	Relative response (dB)
10 kHz	-10
20	-10
50	-9.5
100	-8.8
200	-6.8
500	-2.0
1 MHz	+1.4
2	+2.8
5	+3.6

To avoid deterioration of the baseband signal, the energy dispersal signal is synchronized with the television frame frequency—30 Hz for NTSC signals or 25 Hz for PAL. It is typically a sawtooth waveform having an amplitude that produces a 1 MHz peak-to-peak frequency deviation of the carrier. In a variation of this standard, the deviation is automatically increased to 2 MHz when no video signal is present to provide adequate energy dispersal under no-signal conditions. At the receiver, the energy-dispersal signal is removed by the signal processing circuits.

4.2.1.4 Carrier Generation

In a typical FM exciter design, the carrier is generated at an IF frequency of 70 MHz. The 70 MHz carrier is modulated with the video baseband and audio subcarriers. This frequency will be shifted upward to the final carrier frequency by means of the upconverter. The output of the upconverter feeds the *high-power amplifier,* which provides the final amplification of the signal for transmission (see Figure 1.4).

Para. 25.202(e) of the FCC Rules requires that the frequency stability of the carrier generator be maintained within ± 0.001 percent.

The carrier frequency is typically adjustable in steps of 125 kHz for C band and 500 kHz for Ku band.

4.2.1.5 Audio Subcarriers

The program audio and auxiliary audio channels, for example, cue circuits, for television service are transmitted by means of frequency modulated subcarriers added to the video baseband. Exciters typically provide up to three subcarrier generators at frequencies that can be adjusted from 5.4 to 8.5 MHz. The most commonly used subcarrier frequencies for stereo transmission are 6.2 and 6.8 MHz, but this choice is not universal. See Section 5.4.1.3 for further discussion of the selection of subcarrier frequencies.

Subcarriers can also be used for the transmission of auxiliary audio services.

4.2.1.6 Modulator and Filter

Under current operating practice, video signals are transmitted by satellite in an analog format by means of a frequency modulated carrier. The choice of the modulation index is an important design decision (see Section 5.4.1.2).

The modulated carrier is passed through a filter to eliminate any energy outside the limits established by the choice of modulation index. Exciters typically offer a choice of filter bandwidths ranging from 15 to 40 MHz. For C band, 36 MHz is a standard filter bandwidth. For Ku band, 40 MHz is a common bandwidth for single channel per transponder operation, while 24 MHz is standard for dual channel.

Audio signals for radio service may be transmitted in either an analog or digital format, FM is the modulation mode for analog signals while some form of *phase-shift keying* (PSK) is usually used for digital.

4.2.2 Digital Modulation

The advantages of digital modulation were described in Section 1.1.4.3. They include the capability for virtually noise-free transmission with more channels per transponder than is possible with FM. These features are so valuable that we can expect that satellite transmission of audio and video will change to digital methods as existing equipment gets replaced. New services, such as DBS are already digital.

At the circuit level, digital methods are vastly more complex than analog methods but this complexity can be produced at extremely low cost in integrated circuit devices. The result is that hardware for digital functionality is often less expensive than its analog equivalent. Because of the complexity and also because much digital hardware is *programmable*, there are many options for how digital transmission systems can be constructed. For applications like DBS that involve mass proliferation of equipment, the digital options must be constrained by standardization. However, within well-designed standards, digital systems often provide opportunity for additional processes that may add new features or improve performance without obsoleting equipment already in use.

A complete discussion of digital modulation is beyond the scope of this book. The following presentation covers only some of the ingredients that appear in all digital audio and video systems. A reference[1] offering considerable expansion on the points discussed here is listed on page 73.

4.2.2.1 Analog-to-Digital Conversion

Audio and video signals produced by camera pickup devices and microphones are analog signals. Because of the existing proliferation of analog audio and video equipment, most signals delivered to uplink earth stations are still analog, usually in NTSC or PAL format. This will change in the future as digital cameras and signal systems become more common. That will result in performance improvement because the limitations of analog formats such as NTSC and PAL can be avoided completely. However, until that time, the first step in a digital earth station is analog-to-digital conversion (ADC).

The conversion step is crucial, because it determines the maximum performance capability of the digital system. The conversion parameters of *sampling rate* and *bits per sample* are directly translatable to signal quality factors such as resolution, frequency response, signal-to-noise ratio, etc. Once a signal is in digital form, a system designer (if he or she wishes) can choose to provide perfect transmission. Any compromises in quality are deliberate design decisions (see the next section). Most ADC systems choose the conversion parameters to maintain a nearly *transparent* digital replica of the input, which means that a *digital-to-analog converter* (DAC) connected to the output of the ADC will deliver an analog signal that is subjectively unchanged from the original input.

4.2.2.2 VIdeo Compression

Video signals contain considerable redundancy both spatially and temporally. Digital processing can exploit this redundancy to reduce the amount of data needed for transmission without significantly impairing the picture. This is called *video compression* and it can reduce video data by factors of 20:1 or more. Compression is mandatory in many systems because the raw data rate from a video ADC is so large—100 to 200 Mb/s.

There are many techniques for compression and most systems usually employ several of them. The description of how compression methods are combined into a system is called an *algorithm*. Several of the general compression techniques are:

- *Spatial* compression exploits the similarities that exist in a picture between adjacent picture points (*pixels*). Instead of transmitting every pixel exactly as it comes from the ADC, strategies can be developed for detecting redundancy and removing it from the transmitted bit stream. One of the best methods for doing this is *transform coding*, where blocks of pixels are processed (transformed) to a different representation that will facilitate removal of redundancy. The most popular transform coding is known as the *discrete cosine transform* (DCT). It transforms a block of pixels to a corresponding data block that represents frequency coefficients instead of actual pixel values. Compression is then accomplished by further processing of the higher-frequency coefficient values to represent them less accurately, on the assumption that higher-frequency components are less visible to a viewer.

- Motion video is transmitted as a series of *frames*, usually 25 to 30 per second. Much of the information is a new frame is likely to be similar to what was in the previous frame, except for what has changed because of motion in the scene. A technique called *motion compensation* can detect the areas of a picture that are changing with time and direct the system to transmit only the changes.

- Compression of a data stream is also possible based on the statistics of the data. Data patterns or values that appear often in the data stream can be encoded by a special (short) symbol of bits. Less-probable data patterns are encoded by longer symbols. One common method for this is known as *Huffman coding*.

Many algorithms have been developed by combining these and other techniques. One that has been carefully standardized by the *International Organization for Standardization* (ISO) is called *MPEG*, named for its parent committee: the *Motion Picture Expert Group*. MPEG has several variations, designed for different services; the one most applicable to satellite transmission is MPEG-2. This provides high-quality transmission of standard-definition (525 and 625 lines) signals and low-cost integrated circuits are available to perform MPEG-2 decoding.

It is a property of many compression algorithms that the encode and decode may differ considerably in their complexity—this is called *assymetry*. MPEG is an asymmetric algorithm and the MPEG-2 encode-side processing is very expensive. For satellite transmission, this is not a problem because the encoding is done at the uplink, where an expensive process can be tolerated. Only the decode process has to be done at the viewer's location.

4.2.2.3 Audio Compression

Digital audio signals do not have as much redundancy as video but there is still potential for compression. Compression factors up to about 4:1 are easy to obtain with algorithms that exploit the redundancy between adjacent audio samples. One such algorithm is *adaptive differential pulse code modulation* (ADPCM), which is used in personal computer systems.

Greater compression factors for audio are possible by processing that operates on the frequency spectrum of audio signals; these processors are complex and require custom integrated circuits.[2]

4.2.2.4 Error Protection

The output of an MPEG-2 encoder is a bit stream at a data rate corresponding to the input data rate and the degree of compression. A typical rate for standard-definition video might be 10 Mb/s. When this bit stream is transmitted, there is always some probability of error that will depend on the nature and quality of the transmission system. This is expressed in terms of a *bit error rate* (BER), which is the reciprocal of the number of bits (on the average) that can be transmitted before a single error occurs. It is expressed as a negative power of 10. For example, if the 10 Mb/s bit stream mentioned above had about one error per second, its BER would be 10^{-7}. Compressed audio and video systems require BERs in the range of 10^{-6} to 10^{-9} for subjectively error-free performance.

It is an important advantage of digital transmission systems that errors can be detected and corrected. Detection occurs in two levels:

1. The existence of an error is detected but it is not known where it is; and
2. An error is detected and its location is known. In this case, the error is corrected by simply reversing the value of the error bit.

Error protection is achieved by processing the input bit stream ahead of transmission to add additional "overhead" bits that create patterns to be tested after transmission. If the output processor finds the patterns to be incorrect, it uses that information to locate and correct errors. It is usually convenient to break the bit stream into blocks for error protection and add overhead bits to each block. There are many algorithms for digital error protection; one of the most popular is *Reed-Solomon* coding. A well-designed error protection system can improve a raw BER of 10^{-4} to better than 10^{-9} with the addition of less than 20 percent overhead.

4.2.2.5 Packetizing

A single bit stream is capable of transmitting more than one signal by *multiplexing* the bits of each signal into the main stream. One of the best ways to do this uses the same blocking strategy mentioned above for error protection. The bit stream of each signal is divided into blocks, called *packets*; usually (but not always) packets are all the same size. Error protection is added to each packet and then an additional set of *header* bits is appended. The packets are interleaved one after another into a single bit stream for transmission—this is a form of *time division multiplexing* (TDM). The header bits serve to identify the signal content of the packets so that a receiving device can demultiplex the packets into the original separate bit streams.

Because each packet carries its own identification, the interleaving of packets does not have to have any particular pattern. In some packetizing systems, headers even contain *sequence bits*, which means that packets don't have to be transmitted in the proper order—the receiving device can use the sequence bits to re-order the packets after they are received. This feature is important in terrestrial networks where different packets may travel by different paths but it is usually not needed in satellite communication.

In digital television transmission, separate streams of packets are generated for each video and each audio channel. Packets can be interleaved for multiple channels until their total data rate equals the channel data rate. The flexibility of this approach even allows the number of channels or the data rates of individual channels to change dynamically during transmission.

4.2.2.6 Channel Coding

The bits in a bit stream have only two values: 0 or 1. Depending on the information content of a bit stream, its frequency spectrum may cover an extremely wide range from nearly zero to approximately one-half the maximum data rate. This spectrum could be modulated onto an FM carrier and sent over a satellite link. However, that does not match the satellite capabilities very well and results in a maximum data rate that is substantially less than one-half the bandwidth of the satellite transponder. Optimal digital transmission requires the choice of a modulation method that fits the characteristics of the transmission link.

Using a different modulation method to place the bit stream on a carrier for satellite transmission can boost the maximum data rate of the channel to twice the satellite bandwidth or even higher. The most popular method is known as *quaternary phase shift keying* (QPSK), which can operate over existing satellite transponders. This method is a form of phase modulation and uses four different carrier phases to represent the values of two bits at a time. This is usually obtained by modulating two carriers of the same frequency that are in quadrature (90° phase) with each other. Using QPSK, a 36 MHz satellite channel can carry digital data at 60 Mb/s.

4.2.3 Signal Security

Satellite signals are broadcast over large areas and they are potentially receivable by anyone who has an antenna and a suitable receiver. However, there are many situations where the operator of a video or audio service must restrict his signals only to people who are authorized to receive them. For example, many services obtain their revenue from subscribers who pay for the signals they receive. This does not work unless reception of signals is limited only to those who pay. The solution is to modify the audio and video signals so they cannot be viewed by someone who has just ordinary equipment. This is called *scrambling* the signals. Only paying subscribers are allowed to have equipment suitable to receive the signals. There are many ways to do this and they vary in the amount of security they provide, their flexibility, and their cost.[3]

4.2.3.1 Security Objectives

The objectives of a signal security system may be described as follows:

1. The level of security provided must be consistent with the value of the service and the extent to which unauthorized "hacking" is acceptable. Scrambling systems are sometimes rated on a scale from *soft* (easy to break) to *hard* (difficult to break.)
2. The cost of providing security must be affordable by broadcasters and viewers. In general, more secure systems are more costly, although the curve has changed somewhat with the transition to digital technology.
3. The scrambling system should not noticeably compromise the picture or sound quality available to authorized viewers.
4. Many systems require levels of addressability to support different classes of service on the same system. This is necessary for premium and pay-per-view services. The system should operate in such a way that the viewer is not aware of its existence unless he or she wishes to change his level of service.

Scrambling systems generally require special equipment at the broadcasting site and at the viewer's location. The principal components of a scrambling system are:

1. a data bank that stores the names of the authorized viewers, their address codes, and the level of service they qualify for;
2. equipment for scrambling the video and audio signals before they are uplinked to the satellite;
3. equipment at the viewer's location to provide descrambling only of signals that the viewer is authorized to receive; and
3. a means to transmit enabling signals to authorized descramblers. This may take many forms including (and sometimes in combination): digital codes embedded in the satellite signal, codes sent to the receiving locations by telephone, and mailed-out codes or smart cards. This part of the system is the most critical one to protect from unathorized access.

The following sections describe a few of the more popular scrambling systems in use.

4.2.3.2 The VideoCipher II+ Scrambling System

The VideoCipher® systems were initially developed by General Instruments Corporation and have gone through several versions as a result of field experience over more than ten years. The current version is VideoCipher II+ and it is widely used for cable TV satellite transmissions. Backyard-dish viewers must subscribe to a system that provides a VideoCipher II+ descrambler and the necessary keys to operate it.

VideoCipher II+ employs relatively unsophisticated analog modifications of the video signal in combination with digital audio. Video security is achieved by removing the normal analog synchronizing signals and inverting the video content so that a standard receiver cannot reconstruct the image.

The scrambling of the audio signal is more secure than that of the video. It is converted to digital form and encoded with a digital encryption system (DES). The resulting digital pulse train is transmitted during the vertical blanking interval of the video signal. The descrambler includes a D/A converter for the audio.

As noted in Section 2.5.6, the security of the early VideoCipher system was frequently compromised, and a number of features were added to VideoCipher II+ to make it more resistant to pirates. The encryption elements are all contained in a VLSI (very-large-scale-integrated) circuit that can be replaced with a revised version from time-to-time if necessary. The capacity of the system was also increased from 5 to 50 million subscribers.

Descramblers *are enabled* (authorized) to operate on specific channels by an encoded digital control signal transmitted from the satellite to the earth stations. The control signal contains two levels of selective addressability, both of which must be received to activate the descrambler. The first is a continuous signal that is received by all the VideoCipher descramblers; the second is a periodic signal that provides authorizations for specific earth stations.

The control signal is generated by the DBS Authorization Center (see Section 2.5.6) and transmitted by satellite or telephone line to the uplinks used by the program suppliers. These uplinks, in turn, transmit the control signals to the subscriber earth stations. The DBS Authorization Center maintains a data bank of all authorized subscribers that it receives from the NRTC or other authorized marketing organization.

VideoPal® is a further development of VideoCipher that permits descrambling to be authorized on an individual program basis for pay-per-view systems.

4.2.3.3 B-MAC

Private television systems that have control over the equipment at both ends of the link do not have to follow the standard NTSC or PAL standards. The B-MAC standard is an option in such cases—it provides better picture quality and it is inherently scrambled in that it is a totally different format that cannot be received by standard receivers.

The multiplexed analog components (MAC) approach performs time compression on each line of each component signal so they can be then transmitted sequentially in the normal time of a line. This is a form of *time-division multiplexing* (TDM) and it is responsible for the improved picture quality compared to NTSC or PAL. In B-MAC, further scrambling is added by inserting random delays on a line basis and removing the normal synchronization information. Audio signals are digitized and encrypted. Up to six high-fidelity audio channels can be transmitted along with the video.

Access control in B-MAC is provided by transmitting codes during the blanking intervals. These can be changed at random times by the system operator.

4.2.3.4 The Leitch Digital Scrambling System

Broadcast network programs are not intended to be received directly from the satellite by the general public, and the potential number of authorized earth stations is much lower than for cable TV programs that are also received by backyard dishes. This makes it economical to employ a hard scrambling system.

The Leitch scrambler first converts the incoming analog video signal to a digital format (A/D) and stores it in a memory. The digital signals in the memory are arranged in blocks of 120 lines, and the sequence of the lines as they are read out of the memory is randomly intermixed in accordance with a control data signal. The digital signal is then reconverted to analog form using a DAC, for transmission over the satellite.

The inverse process occurs at the descrambler. The signal is passed through an A/D converter and stored in a memory; and the original line sequence is restored by the control data signal, which is transmitted simultaneously with the video. The control signal also provides the basis for selective addressability, that is, determining which earth stations are authorized to receive the program.

The security of the system depends on the security of the encryption of the control signal. This is enhanced by providing seven alternative super-encrypted keys installed in the descrambler, any one of which may be called up by the control signal.

As with VideoCipher, the audio signal is converted to digital form, encrypted by random alteration of time sequence, and transmitted as a QPSK (quaternary phase shift keying) subcarrier on the video signal.

4.2.3.5 The Videocrypt Digital Scrambling System

The scrambling and encryption system used by the DIRECTV and USSB DBS systems is called Videocrypt. It was originally developed by News Datacom of Israel and Thomson Consumer Electronics. Since the DBS systems employ digital video compression, which is already a form of encryption, the major focus needs to be on the method of access control.

The DBS receiver units utilize a *smart card*, which is a credit-card-sized plastic card containing a microprocessor and memory. The cards are provided on an individual-subscriber basis from the system vendor and contain the appropriate keys required to decode the channels purchased by the subscriber. This card is inserted into a slot in the DBS receiver unit, where the video and audio data pass through the card for access control. The system vendor may issue new cards at any time to modify the algorithm to discourage hackers.

4.3 UPLINK EARTH STATIONS

Figure 1.4 is a block diagram of an uplink earth station. In addition to the antenna, its principal components are a signal scrambler (optional), a signal processor, an up-converter/IPA, and a high-power amplifier (HPA).

Uplink earth stations may be either fixed or portable. Portable earth stations usually operate in the Ku band. Ku-band earth stations employ smaller antennas because of the shorter wavelength, and Ku-band satellite systems do not share frequency allocations with terrestrial microwave systems. Thus, the earth station can be set up on short notice, for a major news event for example, without concern about interference with existing microwave systems.

4.3.1 Uplink Signal Processing

The signal processor is the heart of the uplink earth station electronics; it performs the functions described in Section 4.2. Its output feeds the upconverter, which upconverts the IF carrier to the uplink frequency and raises the power level enough to drive the high-power amplifier (HPA).

4.3.2 High-Power Amplifiers (HPAs)

The power level of the output of the upconverter is typically of the order of one milliwatt, and the HPA must amplify this low-level signal to several hundred watts or even kilowatts to provide sufficient radiated power from the uplink antenna to result in adequate drive at the transponder of the satellite.

A number of different power devices have been used for the final HPA amplifier stage, and the range of choices has broadened with the progress of technology.

The earliest options were klystrons and travelling wave tubes. Klystrons were capable of higher power, but their bandwidth was limited to a single channel. Travelling wave tubes (TWTAs) have bandwidths in excess of 500 MHz and can be used in systems in which more than one channel is amplified by a single HPA. TWTA power output was limited in the early years of satellite communications, but technical advances have increased their power capability significantly.

Advances in solid state technology have made solid state amplifiers (SSPAs) a strong contender in recent years.

It is a frequent practice to operate two HPAs in parallel at half-power and driven from a common source. This provides a degree of redundancy in the event of failure of one of the units and also prolongs their life.

4.3.3 Uplink Performance Specifications

The basic uplink performance specifications are the following: antenna directivity and gain, the HPA power, and the transmission parameters—which include bandwidth, frequency response, and linearity.

The antenna directivity must meet the FCC requirements as stated in Table 4.2.

Ideally, the uplink EIRP, the product of the antenna gain and HPA power, should be sufficient to drive the satellite transponders to saturation (see Section 3.3.2.5). The required EIRP depends on the characteristics of the satellite, but a typical value is 83 dBW. Achieving this EIRP from a single HPA may not be practical in a mobile truck because of constraints on antenna size and power availability (see Chapter 5).

The transmission parameters should be consistent with the Electronic Industries Association (EIA) video and audio system performance standards for satellite systems, EIA/TIA-250. See Tables 15 and 16 in Chapter 5. These standards are for the complete system, and the uplink alone should perform to tighter tolerances.

4.4 DOWNLINK EARTH STATION EQUIPMENT

Figure 1.5 is a block diagram for a typical downlink earth station. Its principal components, in addition to the antenna, are a low-noise amplifier (LNA) and downconverter, or low-noise block converter (LNB); an IF amplifier and demodulator; a signal processor; and a descrambler (if required).

4.4.1 Downlink Received-Noise Performance

Noise* in the received signal affects FM and digital systems differently. In an FM system, received-signal noise contributes directly to the SNR of the output video signal (see Section 5.3.4). In a digital system, received-signal noise has no affect on the video performance if it is below the threshold of the error-protection system. When error protection is effective, the video SNR is determined only by the parameters of the original ADC.

Received-signal noise is largely determined by the specifications of the downlink earth station. Making the optimal trade-off between earth station cost and system noise performance is an essential step in the selection of downlink earth station equipment.

---

* The term *noise* is used in communications systems to describe any unwanted electrical disturbance. It had its origin in telephony where these disturbances produced audible noise in the signal. Its use was continued in video transmission even though it produces no audible effect. In television, the visual effect of noise is *snow* in the picture.

With digital modulation, the video SNR does not vary with the received signal level. Once the signal exceeds the threshold of the digital error protection system, SNR remains constant at the design value (see Section 4.4.6).

A satisfactory SNR is more difficult to achieve with satellites than with microwave systems because earth station receivers must operate with much weaker signals from distant satellites. On the other hand, microwave systems are more subject to atmospheric fading. Thus, the SNR is the more important specification for a satellite circuit, while the fade margin is more important for microwave links.

4.4.2 G/T, the Figure of Merit

Other factors being equal, the noise performance of a downlink earth station is proportional to the ratio G/T, sometimes called the figure of merit, where G is the gain of the antenna and T is the *noise temperature* of the system, a quantity derived from the *noise figure,* F_N.

4.4.2.1 Noise Figure

The noise figure criterion was originally developed for specifying the performance of radar receivers. It is defined as the ratio of the SNR at the output of a receiver to the SNR at its input when the input is at room temperature, T_O (T_O is assumed to be 290°K or 17°C):

$$\text{Noise figure} = F_N = (SNR)_{output}/(SNR)_{input} \qquad (4.1)$$

The noise figure is a satisfactory criterion for systems in which the receiver is the only significant noise contributor, and it is still sometimes used to specify the performance of backyard-dish receivers. Noise temperature has generally replaced noise figure for calculating the performance of satellite systems because it simplifies the calculation of the combined noise contribution of all system components.

4.4.2.2 Noise Temperature

Most of the noise in a properly operating satellite communication system is *random,* with the same characteristics as *thermal noise,* the electrical or electromagnetic signals generated by a hot object. Although some of the noise in a satellite system is non-thermal in origin, it is useful to define an *equivalent noise temperature* that is applied to all system components. It is an expression of noise power (see Appendix A.4 for the relationship between noise temperature and noise power), and is defined as the temperature at which a hot body would generate or emit thermal noise power equal to that generated or emitted by the component, whether thermal or non-thermal in origin.

The noise temperature, T, is specified in degrees Kelvin (°K), its elevation above absolute zero or −273°C. Thus °K = °C +273°. The noise temperature can indicate either the noise power at a point in the system or the ratio of the noise powers at the output and input of a system component. In either case it is proportional to the

Table 4.5 Typical Antenna Noise Temperatures

Elevation angle	C band	Ku band
5°	58°K	80°K
10°	50°K	58°K
30°	30°K	38°K

noise power, and a low noise temperature is desirable. When applied to a component, the output noise power must be *referred* to the input, that is, adjusted for the power loss (as in a waveguide) or the power gain (as in an amplifier) of the component.

The relationship between the noise temperature, T, and the noise figure, F is as follows:

$$T=T_0(F_N-1) \tag{4.2}$$

where $T_0= 290°K$ and F_N is expressed as an arithmetic (not logarithmic) ratio. Because of its universality, the noise temperature is an important specification for most of the equipment components in a satellite downlink.

The use of the ratio, G/T, in calculating the system signal-to-noise ratio is described in Section 5.3.

4.4.3 Receiving Antenna Noise Temperature

The antenna system is one of the sources of electrical noise in a satellite receiving system, but the antenna itself is a minor source of noise. Most of the noise in the antenna output is thermal noise radiated by the earth and atmosphere. Satellite antennas can minimize atmospheric noise by their directivity and a sufficiently high elevation angle. This keeps the main beam well above the earth and shortens its path through the atmosphere (see Table 4.5).

It is usually undesirable to operate Ku-band antennas at elevation angles of less than 10° because of the relatively high noise temperature of the earth and atmosphere and the high signal attenuation during rainstorms at low angles.

4.4.4 Earth Station Input Stages

Figure 1.5 showed a block diagram of the input stages of a downlink earth station. The LNA is combined with a downconverter to form a low-noise block down converter (LNB). The LNB amplifies the signal and shifts its frequency downward to the first IF frequency, usually 950-1450 MHz. At this frequency, a coaxial cable rather than a waveguide can be used for the connection to the receiver.

Table 4.6 Typical LNA Noise Figures and Temperatures

LNA Type	C band		Ku band	
	F_N	T	F_N	T
Field effect transistor	1.1	85°	1.8	150°
Parametric amplifier	0.8	60°	1.5	120°
Cooled parametric amplifier	0.4	29°	0.6	43°

The LNB is located near the antenna. This results in optimum performance because the signal is amplified before it suffers the attenuation loss of the waveguide or transmission line connecting the antenna to the receiver.

The noise temperature of an LNA or the LNA portion of an LNB is determined both by its design and the actual ambient temperature. Great progress has been made in the performance of LNAs in the past decade as the result of improvements in solid state components. *Field effect transistors* using gallium arsenide (GaAsFET) are commonly used in the LNAs of medium-priced earth stations, and a circuit known as a *parametric amplifier* can be used for higher performance. Still higher performance can be achieved by cooling the amplifier. Table 4.6 shows typical LNA noise figures and noise temperatures.

The LNA or LNB is perhaps the most critical element in determining the performance of a receiving system, and its cost/performance trade-off is an important decision in earth station design. The noise temperature of commercially available units varies widely, from 200° or more for low-cost backyard dishes to 25° or less for the costly units used in major satellite carrier earth stations.

4.4.5 Receiver

4.4.5.1 Downconverter

The downconverter heterodynes the carrier-frequency output of the LNA down to an IF frequency. It is the functional equivalent of the first detector or mixer in a broadcast receiver. A frequency synthesizer is often used as the local oscillator for tuning the receiver.

The downconverter can be located either in the receiver or it can be combined with the LNA at the antenna to form an LNB as shown in Figure 1.5. In the latter case, a second downconversion is usually employed to produce a lower intermediate frequency, for example, 70 or 230 MHz.

4.4.5.2 IF Amplifier

The IF bandwidth should be chosen to match the bandwidth occupied by the carrier and its sidebands. This, in turn, is determined by the modulation method. Since the carrier-to-noise ratio is inversely proportional to the IF bandwidth, the bandwidth should be no wider than necessary to accommodate the carrier and its sidebands.

Some receivers have adjustable IF bandwidths that can be optimized for different uplink modulation methods. Others have fixed bandwidths. For C-band receivers, typical values are 32 and 22 MHz. For Ku-band receivers, typical values are 40 MHz for single-channel per transponder FM transmissions, 20 MHz for dual-channel per transponder FM, and 24 MHz for digital DBS.

The term *effective noise bandwidth* is sometimes used to define the bandwidth of the IF amplifier. This is the bandwidth of hypothetical amplifier with uniform response in its pass band and sharp cut-off at the band edges that has the same noise output as the amplifier being specified.

The gain of the IF amplifier must be sufficient to properly drive the demodulator even with the lowest amplitude input signals. Further, its noise temperature should be low enough so that it contributes negligable noise to that already present in the input signal.

4.4.5.3 Demodulator and Signal Processor

An FM demodulator uses a limiter to provide a signal output that is free of residual amplitude modulation and is constant, in spite of wide variations in modulation and input level. The elimination of residual amplitude modulation may generate additional sidebands, and the bandwidth of the output circuit must be wide enough to accommodate these. If it is not, other amplitude modulated components will be regenerated.

A digital QPSK demodulator does not employ a limiter but it must have other means to control the signal level. This usually is in the form of an *automatic gain control* (AGC) loop involving the IF amplifier.

An FM demodulator provides an output voltage that is proportional to the frequency of the input. Some FM demodulators have *threshold extenders* that permit the receiver to operate properly with relatively weak signals. Digital QPSK demodulators generally provide two outputs, representing the bit streams for the two quadrature carriers.

An FM signal processor removes the signal predistortions that were deliberately introduced in the uplink, such as frequency preemphasis and energy dispersal. It also filters extraneous RF signals that may have passed through the demodulator.

A digital signal processor has far more to do because it must perform the error protection processing and demultiplex the packets to reproduce the original bit streams for all the channels. Then, it must decompress the bit streams and use DAC to recover the original analog signals.

4.4.6 Receiver Threshold

For FM, the signal-to-noise ratio of the demodulated video or audio signal, SNR, declines with the SNR of the carrier, CNR, until a critical point is reached, the *receiver threshold,* For values of CNR below threshold, SNR declines rapidly, and the signal becomes unusable. Digital QPSK receivers also have a threshold, caused by the deterioration of raw BER with signal level. When the raw BER exceeds the capability of the error protection system, the system rapidly fails. With raw BER below the threshold, errors are not subjectively observable in the output.

The receiver threshold is a function of its design, and it is an important receiver specification. Typically it occurs at a CNR of 10 dB, for both FM and digital receivers. Some FM demodulators have *threshold extenders* that lower the CNR threshold.

4.5 AUXILIARY EQUIPMENT

In addition to the basic earth station equipment described above, a wide variety of auxiliary equipment is available. They include test equipment, remote control and monitoring equipment, and automatic redundancy switches.

4.5.1 Test Equipment

An earth station should have available all the standard test equipment, such as signal generators and oscilloscopes, which are required for communication systems operating in the gigahertz frequency range. In addition, uplink stations should have three specialized types of equipment available: a spectrum analyzer, a signal level meter, and a loop test translator.

4.5.1.1 Spectrum Analyzer

A spectrum analyzer is perhaps the most useful type of test equipment for the initial setup and maintenance of an uplink. As its name implies, it displays the amplitude of the signals in a circuit as a function of frequency over a specified frequency range. It is not inexpensive—its cost ranges from $15,000 to $60,000, depending on the frequency range and other features—but a unit satisfactory for use in uplink installation and maintenance can be obtained near the bottom of this range.

Among other applications, the spectrum analyzer can be used to identify a specific satellite during the installation of an earth station. It can be used to adjust the carrier frequency and modulation index of an uplink channel. Similarly, it can be used to adjust the frequency and modulation index of an audio subcarrier. It can be used to adjust the amplitude of an energy dispersal waveform. It is an extremely versatile unit.

4.5.1.2 Signal Level Meter

A signal level meter, calibrated for CNR measurements, is required for routine checks of the CNR—a basic criterion of the performance of a satellite system.

4.5.1.3 Loop Test Translator

The loop test translator makes it possible to test the linearity and frequency response of a complete uplink/downlink earth station without passing the signal through the satellite. See Section 7.5.2 for a description of its operation.

4.5.2 Remote Control and Monitoring Equipment

Equipment is available for the remote control and monitoring of a variety of earth station functions.

Remote control equipment on the market covers a wide range of costs and the extent of control functions. A simple system provides facilities for the remote control of antenna azimuths and elevations. At the other extreme are computer driven systems provided with a screen that can display such information as block diagrams of the earth station subsystems, status and fault indicators for all components, and the elevation and azimuth of a number of satellites. They can also include automatic monitoring equipment such as a logging printer and alarms.

4.5.3 Automatic Redundancy Switches

Earth stations operating in systems that have high requirements for reliability usually have redundant, that is, spare, equipment components, which can be switched into use in the event of failure to the main component. Equipment is available which makes the switchover automatic.

If the system includes several channels, it is normal practice to provide only one redundant unit for all channels, on the assumption that it is very unlikely that two or more channels would fail simultaneously. If one redundant or backup unit is protecting N channels, it is known as 1:N protection. The redundancy switch equipment detects the failed channel and automatically switches the backup component into operation.

4.5.4 Special Equipment for Mobile Stations

Certain special equipment and facilities are required for mobile stations or trucks.

A good magnetic compass for orienting the truck with respect to magnetic north is an obvious requirement.

A truck stabilizer is necessary to establish and maintain the level of the antenna mounting structure within small tolerances.

It is essential to provide facilities for telephone communication with the satellite control center at the signal receiving point, such as a broadcast station master control. This system can employ a combination of a cellular telephone and a two-way satellite circuit. The complexity of remote telephone systems sometimes exceeds that of the signal transmission system.

Notes

1   Luther, A. C., *Digital Audio and Video*, Artech House, Norwood, MA, 1997.

2   Pohlmann, K. C., *Principles of Digital Audio*, McGraw-Hill, New York, 1995.

3   For a summary of scrambling techniques that provide security for video signals, see Inglis, A.F., *Electronic Communication Handbook,* Chapter 17, McGraw-Hill, New York, 1988.

5

Station Planning

This chapter describes the design practices that are applicable to the earth station types commonly used for the transmission and distribution of radio and television programming. They include the following:

1. TVROs for CATV head-ends and broadcast stations
2. Uplinks for CATV program suppliers
3. Uplinks for specialized and ad hoc broadcast networks, and for program syndication
4. Portable ENG (electronic news gathering) stations
5. TVROs for low-cost backyard dishes
6. DBS receivers

5.1 PERFORMANCE AND RELIABILITY SPECIFICATIONS

Establishing the desired specifications for system performance and availability is an essential first step in the design of satellite earth stations. It involves a careful consideration of the trade-offs between system cost, electrical performance, and reliability. This section describes commonly accepted industry standards for performance and availability that can serve as guidelines for earth station design.

5.1.1 Television Transmission System Performance Standards

The Electronic Industries Association (EIA) electrical performance standards for television transmission systems as stated in its publication, EIA/TIA-250-C,[1] "Electrical Performance Standards for Television Transmission Systems," are commonly accepted industry standards for analog video and audio circuits.

EIA/TIA-250-C establishes performance specifications for six circuit lengths:

Short-haul	Less than 20 route miles
Medium-haul	20 to 150 route miles
Satellite	Independent of circuit length
Long-haul	Over 150 route miles
End-to-end	Complete circuit from source to end point

75

The video performance standards for the different circuit lengths reflect the relative difficulty in achieving them. For example, the specifications for satellite circuits are more stringent than for long-haul circuits because the latter are assumed to require a number of repeaters in tandem, each contributing additional degradation of signal quality. On the other hand, the SNR specification for satellite circuits (56 dB, weighted) is not as stringent as for short-haul terrestrial circuits (67 dB) or medium-haul circuits (60 dB). These considerations do not necessarily apply to digital transmission systems because degradations usually do not accumulate in cascaded digital circuits.

The audio performance standards are the same for all circuit lengths with the exception of the SNR, which is 2 dB less for end-to-end circuits.

The principal EIA/TIA-250-C transmission specifications for video and audio signals are summarized in Tables 5.1 and 5.2. This document also defines the parameters used to specify transmission performance and describes the procedures for measuring them.

The video SNR and system availability are the most critical of these specifications because they have a major effect on G/T and other factors affecting the cost of

Table 5.1 EIA/TIA-250-C Analog Video Performance Standards

Parameter	Satellite	End-to-end
Gain/frequency distortion		
200kHz (reference)	0.0dB	0.0dB
50 Hz to 150 kHz	±0.2dB	±0.3dB
At 3 MHz	±0.7dB	±1.0dB
3.3 to 39MHz	±0.35dB	±0.55dB
At 4.2 MHz	±0.65dB	±1.2dB
Chrominance-luminance gain inequality	±4 IRE	±7 IRE
Chrominance-luminance delay inequality	±26 ns	±60 ns
Field-time waveform distortion, p to p	3 IRE	3 IRE
Line-time waveform distortion. p to p	1 IRE	2 IRE
Short-time waveform distortion	2%	3%
Insertion gain variation with time	±0.2 dB	±0.5dB
Luminance nonlinearity	6%	10%
Differential gain	4%	1%
Differential phase	1.5 deg	3 deg
Chrominance-luminance intermodulation	2 IRE	4 IRE
Chrominance nonlinear gain distortion	2 IRE	5 IRE
Chrominance nonlinear phase distortion	2 deg	5 deg
SNR, weighted	56 dB	54 dB

downlink earth stations. The performance of current systems, which often falls short of these standards, is described in more detail later in the chapter.

Note that the SNR standard is based on *weighted* noise. *Noise weighting* is used to estimate the perceived visual effect of the noise, and is based on the fact that the fine-grained noise generated by high frequency components is not as visible to the eye as the coarser noise generated by lower frequencies.

Noise weighting is accomplished by multiplying the noise frequency spectrum by a curve representing the relative response of a "normal" eye to noise components of different frequencies under a specified set of conditions. EIA/TIA-250-C specifies a standard weighting curve for 525 line NTSC systems, which is based on a viewing ratio (ratio of viewing distance to picture height) of 4.

The difference between the unweighted and weighted S/N expressed in decibels is known as the *noise weighting factor*. Weighted noise does not represent noise power but rather is an approximate measure of its visibility. The equivalent unweighted SNR, based on the actual noise power, is calculated by subtracting the noise weighting factor from the weighted SNR.

11 dB is the approximate noise weighting factor for NTSC FM systems, and this results in an unweighted SNR standard of 45 (56–11) dB for satellite circuits and 43 dB for end-to-end circuits that include a frequency modulated link. This is a conservative standard, and at this level the noise is virtually invisible.

If the viewing ratio is reduced, for example, to 3 times picture height, as has been proposed for HDTV, the noise weighting factor must be reduced correspondingly because fine-grained noise becomes more visible. The amount of reduction depends on the scanning standards of the HDTV system, but a 5 dB reduction would be typical. This would increase the unweighted SNR standard to 50 (45+5) dB.

In digital systems, the principal noise source is the quantizing noise of the ADC, which does not increase with signal frequency like FM noise. This means that the noise weighting factor for digital modulation is lower. Fortunately, digital systems are usually designed to have very high ADC SNR, so the noise weighting issue is not very important.

Table 5.2 EIA/TIA-250-C Satellite and End-to-End Audio Performance Standards

Amplitude-frequency response	
400 Hz (reference)	0 dB
At 50 Hz	-1.0 ±0.5 dB
100 to 7,500 Hz	±0.5dB
At 15,000 Hz	-1.5 ±0.5 dB
Total harmonic distortion	0.5 percent
SNR (weighted)	58 dB*

* Specification for satellite link; end-to-end specification is 56 dB.

5.1.2 FM Radio Transmission System Performance Standards

The audio standards in EIA/TIA-250-C are for the audio portion of a television signal. They would give excellent results for program distribution to FM radio broadcasting stations as well, and they are somewhat more stringent than the FCC standards. There is, however, a desire on the part of some broadcasters for even higher fidelity with stricter standards than those in EIA/TIA-250-C. These can be achieved by digital transmission. For example, harmonic distortion can be limited to 0.3 percent, and a SNR of 60 dB or better can be achieved. The lack of noise in an idle digital channel is particularly impressive, and it can be as much as 80 dB below the reference program level.

5.1.3 Availability Specifications

As with the video SNR, earth station costs are very sensitive to the availability specifications of the system. Maximum availability requires complete equipment redundancy and a large fade margin (see Section 5.3.2), both of which add greatly to the cost. The designer, therefore, must consider carefully the cost of occasional service interruptions and compare it with the cost of a more conservative design.

The need for a high level of availability varies greatly with the application. At one extreme is the transmission of a major event such as the Super Bowl game, with millions of viewers and millions of dollars of revenue at risk with even a short interruption. On the other extreme is a backyard-dish earth station where an occasional interruption is, at worst, an annoyance.

EIA\TIA-250-C specifies signal availability of 99.99 percent. This standard allows cumulative outages of 53 minutes per year from all causes—sun outages, equipment failures, operational errors, and, for Ku band, rain outages. This is a very demanding requirement, and the designer of the system should consider carefully whether its cost is justified.

5.2 EARTH STATION LOCATION

5.2.1 Site Requirements

There are three requirements for an earth station site. They are as follows:

1. There must be a clear line-of-site path to the satellite.
2. The usual requirements for physical access, zoning and land-use restrictions, power availability, and proximity to the source or end point of the signal path must be met. (Under certain conditions the FCC has the authority to preempt state and local zoning regulations. See Para. 25.104 of Part 25 of the FCC Rules.)
3. It must be free of objectionable mutual interference with other terrestrial systems, particularly microwave systems.

The first requirement, a clear line-of-sight path from the earth station site to the satellite or satellites to be accessed, is necessary for all frequency bands and earth station types. The second requirement, compliance with local land-use and zoning ordinances, must be met for all stations. The third requirement, freedom from objectionable mutual interference, which is only of concern at C band, is quite different for licensed and unlicensed downlink earth stations. A licensed downlink station must meet FCC requirements with respect to co-channel interference that are almost as rigid as for uplink stations. The FCC definition of "objectionable" interference is quite severe, and many users are satisfied with the performance of a system that meets less rigid requirements.

5.2.1.1 Line-of-Sight Path

The availability of a line-of-sight path can be checked with a transit after the elevation and azimuth angles of the satellite have been determined. Although the initial requirement may be only to access a single satellite, conservative design practice dictates that there should be a line-of-sight to all orbital slots in the portions of the orbital arc allocated to the country of use (see Chapter 1). Slot assignments may change, or there may be a need in the future to access a different satellite.

Tables may be available showing the angles to orbital slots from the earth station's vicinity, or they can be calculated from the equations in Appendix A.5.

5.2.1.2 Site Clearance—Licensed Stations

The FCC requires that earth station sites for all uplink stations and for licensed downlink stations be *cleared,* that is, that they be coordinated with other users of the same frequency bands. For the Ku band, "other" users are Ku-band earth stations, and for the C band, they include both C-band microwave systems and other C-band earth stations. A new site must be cleared, that is, shown to be free of interference to or from existing and authorized facilities, before it can be licensed. FCC coordination requirements are stated in Paras. 25.201 to 25.204 of Part 25 of its Rules.

A preliminary examination of potential earth station sites can be made by field measurements to determine the existence of interfering signals. After a site has been tentatively selected on this basis, detailed coordination data must be prepared and filed with an application to the FCC (see Section 6.3). Applicants are urged to retain a professional frequency coordinator who is familiar with the FCC Rules and procedures, and who maintains a data base of terrestrial microwave facilities, existing and authorized.

Because of the large number of microwave installations, it is often difficult to find an earth station site in major metropolitan areas that can be completely cleared for C-band, that is, cleared for all channels and all orbital slots. For this reason, the major earth stations operated by satellite carriers are usually located many miles from the city center. Partial clearance, for example, for a single channel or orbital slot, can often be achieved, even in urban areas. Also, advantage can be taken of buildings or natural obstructions that are not listed in the FCC data banks.

5.2.1.3 Site Selection—Unlicensed Stations

The selection of a site for an unlicensed station is based on the field survey steps described earlier. In the case of C-band sites, the owner must make his or her own judgement as to whether the interference on any channels is severe enough to disqualify the site. Criteria for evaluating the severity of co-channel interference and techniques for minimizing it are described later as part of the treatment of downlink earth station design. Ku-band site selection is based only on the line-of-sight requirement.

5.3 SATELLITE LINK CALCULATIONS

The design of earth station facilities requires calculation of the SNR and *fade margin* of the satellite link. The fade margin is the difference between the CNR at the receiver under normal conditions and the receiver threshold (see Section 4.4.6). Calculation of the SNR for frequency modulated systems is carried out in two steps: determining the CNR followed by the conversion of this ratio to SNR.

5.3.1 CNR

The CNR is the ratio of the power of an unmodulated carrier to the noise power. It is given in dB by the equation:

$$CNR = [EIRP - 20\log f - 10\log B_{IF} + 45] + G/T \qquad (5.1)$$

where:

EIRP = the effective isotropic radiated power of the satellite footprint at the downlink receiver location.

f = carrier frequency in GHz

B_{IF} = IF bandwidth in Hz

G/T = gain-to-temperature ratio as defined in Section 4.4.2. G is the gain of the downlink antenna and T is the noise temperature of the system, usually $T_{LNA} + T_{Antenna}$.

Note that the CNR is inversely proportional to the IF bandwidth. In FM systems, this creates the necessity for a trade-off between fade margin and SNR in selecting the modulation index (see below).

5.3.2 Fade Margin

After the calculation of the CNR, the fade margin is easily determined by subtracting the receiver threshold from CNR. An adequate fade margin is particularly important in the Ku band because it should be large enough to offset rain fades.

5.3.3 Rain Fades

Unlike sun outages, rain outages are unpredictable. They are caused not only by the attenuation of the radio wave by water droplets but also by the presence of background sky noise which results from precipitation. Light-to-moderate rain rates do not cause a problem, and outages only occur in torrential rainstorms. Uplinks usually have enough reserve power to overcome rain attenuation, and outages occur mainly in downlinks.

The cumulative outage time depends on the frequency of heavy rainstorms, the earth station fade margin, and the elevation angle of the antenna. As noted earlier, elevation angles of less than 10° are unsatisfactory in the Ku band because of the long path of the beam through the atmosphere. It is fortunate that elevation angles are highest in the southern latitudes of the Gulf states where heavy rains are the most frequent.

Many attempts have been made to develop a method for forecasting availability on a quantitative basis by applying statistical measurement data to theoretical models. The results have not been completely satisfactory, and forecasts at best are order-of-magnitude estimates.

The required fade margin as calculated from these models for very high availability can be impractically large. One model, for example, indicates a fade margin requirement of nearly 40 dB for 99.99 percent availability in the Gulf Coast region. A practical solution in these areas is to make the G/T of the downlinks as high as economically practical and accept the availability that results. There is some evidence that the existing models are unduly pessimistic and that actual experience will be better.

On the basis of information currently available, the following fade margins are suggested for Ku-band circuits in the United States with a high availability requirement and with elevation angles in excess of 20°:

Location	*Suggested fade margin*
Gulf Coast states	16 dB
Other continental United States	13 dB

If an extremely high degree of availability is required, it can be achieved by the use of a C-band backup channel or by a *space diversity* Ku-band earth station installed some distance from the first. Torrential rainstorms that cause fading usually cover only a limited area at any given time, and it is unusual to suffer simultaneous fading at sites separated by a few miles.

5.3.4 SNR

After calculating the CNR, it is converted to the SNR for FM video signals by means of equation 5.2 (all terms are in (dB)):

$$SNR = CNR + F_{DEEMPH} + F_w + F_{FM} \qquad (5.2)$$

where:

CNR is calculated by equation 5.1.

F_{DEEMPH} is the deemphasis factor (see Section 4.2.1.1).

F_w is the noise weighting factor (see Section 5.1.1).

F_{FM} is the FM improvement factor.

F_{FM} is the ratio of the SNR for the demodulated video baseband to the CNR of the unmodulated carrier. For satellite transmission of video signals, it is typically 20 to 30 dB. Its equation is:

$$F_{FM} = 20 \log[\Delta(f_v)/2B_v] + 10 \log[B_{IF}/B_v] + 7 \tag{5.3}$$

where:

B_v is the video bandwidth

B_{IF} is the IF bandwidth

For NTSC transmissions, 12.8 dB is commonly used for the sum of F_{DEEMPH} and F_W. Note that F_{FM} and, hence, the SNR increases as the square of the carrier deviation. Increasing the SNR by this method has the problem that it necessitates an increase in the IF bandwidth and a reduction in the fade margin. As described earlier, the trade-off between fade margin and SNR must be carefully calculated.

5.4 UPLINK EARTH STATION DESIGN

The uplink earth station determines all of the properties of the downlink signal except for the EIRP, which is determined by the satellite. They include the type of modulation, the modulation index for frequency modulation, the bit rate for digital transmission, the RF bandwidth, the use of subcarriers, and the baseband format, that is, analog or digital.

Until recently, the analog format and frequency modulation were used almost exclusively for satellite transmission of television signals, both video and audio. Now, digital transmission of TV signals is growing rapidly. Both digital and analog transmission are used for radio signals.

The downlink earth station determines the SNR and fade margin of the link, within the parameters established by the uplink and the satellite.

5.4.1 Television Service

5.4.1.1 Antenna and HPA

The antenna directivity must be sufficient to meet the FCC Rules, as shown in Table 4.2; and its gain in combination with the HPA power should produce sufficient EIRP to drive a satellite transponder to saturation. The EIRP required to produce saturation is typically 83 dBW. The drive for multiple-carrier transponders is much lower, to avoid excessive intermodulation. Table 5.3 is a tabulation of typical antenna/HPA combinations.

Table 5.3 Typical Antenna Diameter-HPA Combinations

Antenna Diameter	C band	
	7 meters	10 meters
Antenna Gain (dBi)	50.9	53.5
HPA Power (W)	1,000	1,000
Max. EIRP (dBi)	80.9	83.5

Antenna Diameter	Ku band		
	3 meters	5 meters	7 meters
Antenna Gain (dBi)	50.5	55.0	57.5
HPA Power (W)	500	700	1000
Max EIRP (dBi)	77.5	83.5	87.5

The HPA power in Ku-band uplinks can be adjusted, either manually or automatically, by measuring the strength of the downlink signal from the satellite beacon. If attenuation of the signal results from heavy rainfall, the HPA power can be increased to compensate.

5.4.1.2 Modulation Index

In FM systems, the choice of the *modulation index,* the ratio of the peak frequency deviation to the highest baseband frequency component, is a trade-off between the SNR of the system and its fade margin. Increasing the deviation improves the SNR of the receiver output, but requires a wider bandwidth IF amplifier, which increases the RF signal level required to exceed the receiver's threshold.

A typical C-band deviation standard is 21.5 MHz peak-to-peak (P-P), plus 1 MHz for the energy dispersal waveform. The IF bandwidth is 32 MHz.

Although Ku-band transponders have a wider bandwidth than C-band, it is not always prudent to take advantage of this by a larger modulation index. To do so would require a wider IF bandwidth resulting in a lower C/N and a reduced fade margin. An alternative is to utilize the wider Ku-band transponder bandwidth by transmitting two television channels on one transponder. In this mode, a typical peak-to-peak deviation is 18.2 MHz with an IF bandwidth of 24 MHz.

5.4.1.3 Audio Subcarriers

Frequency modulated subcarriers added to the video baseband signal are used to transmit the audio program material and any auxiliary audio channels. Additional subcarriers are sometimes added to carry cue and other communication channels.

The choice of the subcarrier frequency is another trade-off. It must be far enough above the video baseband spectrum so that the two can be separated at the receiver by suitable filters. Also, increasing the subcarrier frequency permits a higher modulation index for the audio signal. The disadvantages are that it increases the bandwidth requirement of the system, reducing the carrier-to-noise ratio and fade margin; and it places the audio subcarrier in a higher noise region of the demodulated signal. The greater bandwidth reduces the CNR and the fade margin. Subcarrier frequencies commonly used are 6.2 and 6.8 MHz, although lower frequencies such as 5.4 MHz are sometimes used in dual-channel Ku-band systems to reduce the required IF bandwidth.

There is no industry standard for the modulation index of the audio subcarrier, and it varies in current systems from the FM broadcast standard of 150 kHz P-P to more than 900 kHz.

5.4.1.4 Mobile Uplinks

The extensive usage of satellite transmission for electronic news gathering and sporting events has created a demand for mobile uplinks or "trucks." Complete packaged uplinks (and downlinks) are now available from a number of manufacturers. These include all the facilities that are required for rapid setup and operation at remote sites that may not have a source of primary power. They are designed by the manufacturer so that the user has only the responsibility of selecting the one that best fills his needs, and, possibly, of specifying custom features.

The constraints on antenna size and HPA power that result from the mobility requirement may make it impossible to achieve a sufficiently high uplink EIRP to provide even one-half the power needed to saturate a transponder. The 3 m, 500 W earth station shown in Table 5.3 is near the top limit for the EIRP of mobile units. Commonly used are 2 m, 300 W units with an EIRP of 73 dBW.

5.4.1.5 Typical Transponder Utilization

For television service, the standard utilization of each 36 MHz satellite channel is one video signal, plus one or more audio signals. For less demanding applications, two television channels, including audio and video, can be transmitted in a single channel by reducing the modulation index. This mode is seldom used at C band, but it is common at Ku band.

Typical transponder utilizations for C-band and Ku-band transmission of television programs are summarized in Table 5.4.

5.4.2 Radio Service

Radio programs are transmitted in both the analog and digital modes.

Table 5.4 Typical Transponder Utilization, Television Transmission (Values in MHz)

	C band One TV channel	Ku band One TV channel	Two TV channels
Transponder bandwidth	36	54	54
IF bandwidth	32	32	24
P-P deviation, video	1.5	21.5	15
Audio subcarrier	6.8	6.8	5.4
P-P deviation, audio	0.9	0.28	0.15

5.4.2.1 Digital Transmission

PSK (phase shift keying) or FSK (frequency shift keying) is used for digital transmission. Several program channels can be multiplexed on a single carrier using time division multiplex (TDM), or a separate carrier can be used for each channel (single channel per carrier, or SCPC).

The major radio networks employ a TDM digital system developed by Scientific Atlanta. This system multiplexes two 15 kHz stereo channels, one 7.5 kHz stereo channel, and two voice cuing channels in a 2.048 Mb/s bit stream. The transmission specifications of this system meet the requirements of high fidelity FM broadcasting stations.

The ability to multiplex cuing signals with the program audio is a feature of this system. This permits remote network control of station switching systems, cartridge recorders, and other functions.

5.4.2.2 Analog Transmission

Regional and specialized radio networks commonly use SCPC transmission with analog transmission and frequency modulation. The signal processing includes standard audio preemphasis and volume compression/expansion to increase the average modulation level. The frequency deviation is typically 150 to 200 kHz P-P.

5.5 DOWNLINK EARTH STATION DESIGN

5.5.1 Licensing

An FCC license is mandatory for uplink earth stations, but it is optional for downlinks.

Licensing has the advantage that the station is given protection against cochannel interference from future microwave and satellite systems. The licensing procedure, however, can be costly and time-consuming (see Chapter 6), and it imposes antenna specifications and site criteria that may be unnecessary.

The result is that very few backyard dishes are licensed. On the other hand, cable TV systems and broadcast stations that depend on the station for their revenue may find it prudent to go through the licensing process for their TVROs.

5.5.2 Design Objectives

The principal design objectives for downlink earth stations are the following:

1. Cost.
2. Freedom from co-channel interference from terrestrial sources, such as microwave systems, and other earth stations, or from adjacent satellites.
3. A satisfactory SNR.
4. An adequate fade margin, particularly for Ku-band stations.

The downlink design parameters that determine the performance against these objectives are the antenna location, the antenna directivity, and the earth station figure of merit, or G/T. The other key link parameters—the downlink EIRP, the modulation method, and the required IF bandwidth—are established by the uplink and the satellite.

5.5.3 Cost

Downlink earth stations come in a wide range of costs, features, and performance. Simple C-band backyard-dish stations may cost less than $2,000. DBS earth stations cost $500 or less.

TVROs for cable TV systems and broadcast TV stations cost from $5,000 to $25,000. DATS TVROs for radio stations cost from $7,000 to $9,000. The cost of the downlink portion of earth stations used by major carriers may exceed $100,000. The cost variables include the antenna diameter, the receiver noise figure, the antenna mounting structure, accessories, operating features, the degree of redundancy, and the general quality of the system components. Establishing the cost/performance trade-off is a critical decision in earth station design.

5.5.4 Co-channel Interference

The earth station licensing requirements as contained in Part 25 of the FCC Rules provide excellent assurance against objectionable co-channel interference. But to take advantage of the additional flexibility permitted in the location and design of unlicensed stations, it is necessary to consider the amount of interference that can be tolerated, the sources of interference, and the steps that can be taken to minimize it, even when it is not possible to meet the FCC licensing requirements.

5.5.4.1 Interference Visibility

As with FM broadcasting, the use of frequency modulation reduces the susceptibility of signals to co-channel interference. Interference begins to be visible at a carrier-to-interfering-carrier ratio (C/I) of 17 to 21 dB. It becomes objectionable, even to an untrained observer, at a C/I of about 9 dB. The FCC criteria for objectionable co-channel interference—28 dB for point-to-point service and 22 dB for point-to-multipoint service—are more stringent.

5.5.4.2 Terrestrial Interference Sources

The most common source of terrestrial co-channel interference in the C-band is microwave systems. They are a particular problem in congested urban areas that are termination points for multiple microwave paths.

The best protection against co-channel interference from microwave systems and other earth stations, of course, is to locate the station in an area that is totally free of interfering signals. If it is not practical to locate the earth station in an interference-free site, successful operation can often be achieved by making use of antenna directivity and the natural shielding provided by buildings or local terrain features. Alternatively, artificial barriers can be constructed. At C band, trees can provide 6 to 10 dB of isolation, earth berms 10 to 15 dB, and wire screens up to 20 dB.[2]

As a last resort, interference from microwave transmitters can be minimized by installing notch filters in the earth station IF amplifier at the microwave carrier frequencies, which are spaced ±10 MHz from the center of the transponder channel. (Such filters are available commercially.) The elimination of the interfering signals is not complete, and the notches degrade the performance somewhat, but the results can be satisfactory for backyard-dish systems.

5.5.4.3 Adjacent Satellites

The earth station must depend on the directivity of its receiving antenna and the suppression of its side lobes to protect it from interference from adjacent satellites. Antennas meeting the directivity standards established by the FCC for uplink antennas (see Table 4.2) will provide excellent discrimination against adjacent-satellite interference. In practice, receiving antennas with lesser directivity often gives satisfactory results, particularly for backyard dishes with their less stringent performance requirements.

5.5.5 SNR Objectives

The EIA standards for SNR shown in Table 5.1 are extremely demanding, and more moderate specifications have been developed by other industry and governmental organizations. Table 5.5 is a representative list of alternative standards. Some are stated in terms of unweighted noise and others in terms of weighted noise. Derived

Table 5.5 SNR Standards

Standardizing organization	Standard for	SNR (dB) weighted	SNR (dB) unweighted
EIA	Satellite link	56	(45)
EIA	End-to-end system	54	(43)
FCC	Cable TV system	(47)	36
TASO*	Broadcast TV		
Grade 1 (Excellent)		(52)	41
Grade 2 (Fine)		(44-52)	33-41
Grade 3 (Passable)		(39-44)	28-33
Grade 4 (Marginal)		(34-39)	23-28
Grade 5 (Inferior)		(28-34)	17-23
Grade 6 (Unusable)		(28)	

* Television Allocations Study Organization

standards, assuming an 11 dB weighting factor for FM systems, are shown in parentheses. This assumes an NTSC system and a viewing ratio of 4.

The wide variation in these standards reflects the highly subjective nature of this aspect of picture quality and the great differences in the tolerance of members of the public to noise.

The weighting factor for HDTV signals is less, typically by 5 dB, than for NTSC systems. With this weighting factor, the HDTV unweighted SNR should be at least 5 dB greater for comparable visual perception.

5.5.6 Availability Objectives

The EIA availability standard of 99.99 percent is extremely difficult to meet, and, in some cases, may be impossible. Even 99.98 percent availability, which allows twice as much outage time, requires system redundancy and places severe demands on equipment reliability and earth station G/T. Such a system can cost twice as much as one with more modest requirements. For most applications, availabilities in the range of 99.5 to 99.8 percent are adequate and much more cost effective.

5.5.7 Earth Station G/T

The ratio G/T is the most basic specification of downlink earth stations because it determines both the SNR and the fade margin (see equations 5.1 and 5.2). It is the ratio, expressed in decibels, of the antenna gain with respect to an isotropic radiator to the system noise temperature in degrees Kelvin (degrees centigrade + 273°). The result is expressed in dBK:

$$(G/T)_{dBK} = G_{dBi} - 10 \log T_K \tag{5.4}$$

5.6 PERFORMANCE OF REPRESENTATIVE SYSTEMS

This section describes the performance of five typical satellite systems used for the transmission or distribution of television signals. They are the following:

1. A high-performance system used for a point-to-point trunk circuit.
2. A system for the distribution of programs to cable TV systems.
3. A mobile Ku-band system for ENG service for a television broadcast station. (This system employs one-half transponder.)
4. A C-band backyard-dish system.
5. A DBS system.

5.6.1 Uplink EIRP

Table 5.6 shows the uplink EIRP performance of representative antenna-HPA combinations. With the exception of the mobile uplink, in which the EIRP is limited by the constraints on antenna size and HPA power and by the sharing of the transponder with another channel, all have capacity in excess of the 83 dBW required to saturate the satellite transponder. They would be operated, therefore, at less than full power. The mobile uplink EIRP could be increased by 3 dB by operating two HPAs in parallel.

5.6.2 Downlink Earth Station G/T

Table 5.7 shows representative G/T values for downlink earth stations.

5.6.3 System C/N and Fade Margin

Table 5.8 shows representative CNR and fade margin performance.

5.6.4 FM Improvement Factor

Table 5.9 shows representative FM improvement factors.

5.6.5 System SNR

Table 5.10 shows the SNR performance (weighted) that is representative of these systems.

Table 5.6 Representative Uplink EIRP Values

	Point-to-point trunk	CATV	ENG	Backyard Dish	DBS
Band	C	C	Ku	C	DBS
Antenna Diameter (m)	10	10	2.5	10	7
Gain (dBi)	54	54	48	54	58
Max. HPA Power					
W	2,000	2,000	500	2,000	2,000
dBW	33	33	27	33	33
Max. Uplink EIRP (dBW)	87	87	75	87	91

Table 5.7 Representative G/T Values—Downlink Stations

	$(G/T)_{dB/K} = G_{dBi} - 10logT_k$				
	Point-to-point trunk	CATV	ENG	Backyard Dish	DBS
Band	C	C	Ku	C	DBS
Antenna Dia.(m)	11	4.5	5	2	0.5
Gain (dBi)	55	42	54	36	34
Noise Temp. (°K)					
Antenna	40	40	50	40	50
LNA	50	85	150	125	150
T_K	90	125	200	165	200
(G/T) (dB/K)	35	21	31	14	11

5.6.6 Backyard Dish Performance

These tables clearly show the compromises which must be made to operate a C-band backyard dish with small antenna.

A weighted SNR of 42 dB produces a picture that is noisy by professional standards, although it appears to be satisfactory to the public, particularly in the absence of competing program availability.

The fade margin of 3 dB is barely adequate, even when high reliability is not required. It is based on an assumed EIRP of 38 dBW at the station site, a threshold extender, and reduced IF bandwidth. Reducing the bandwidth to 24 MHz to improve the fade margin will have an adverse effect on sound and picture quality.

If the EIRP were much less, it would be necessary to install a larger antenna.

Table 5.8 Representative CNR and Fade Margin Values—Downlike Earth Stations

$$(CNR)_{dB} = [EIRP - 20log f_{GHz} - 10log B_{IF} + 45] + (G/T)_{dB/K}$$
$$Fade\ margin = C/N - Receiver\ threshold$$

	Point-to-point trunk	CATV	ENG	Backyard Dish	DBS
Band	C	C	Ku	C	DBS
Downlink EIRP	38	38	43	38	50
f_{GHz}	4	4	12	4	12.5
B_{IF} x10^6 Hz	32	32	24	24	27
G/T (dB/K)	35	21	31	14	11
CNR (dB)	31	17	24	11	12
Recvr Threshold (dB)	12	8	12	8	8
Fade Margin (dB)	19	9	12	3	4

Table 5.9 Representative FM Improvement Factors—Downlink Earth Stations

$$F_{FM} = 20log[\Delta(f_v)/B_v] + 10log[B_{IF}/B_v] + 7$$

	Point-to-point trunk	CATV	ENG	Backyard Dish	DBS
Band	C	C	Ku	C	DBS
B_v (Mhz)	4.2	4.2	4.2	4.2	4.2
B_{IF} (MHz)	32	32	24	24	27
F_{FM}	23.8	23.8	21.5	23.8	22.7

Table 5.10 Representative SNRs (Weighted)

$$S/N = CNR + F_{FM} + F_{DEEMPH} F_{FM}$$
$$F_{DEEMPH} + F_W = 13\ dB$$

	Point-to-point trunk	CATV	ENG	Backyard Dish	DBS
Band	C	C	Ku	C	DBS
CNR (dB)	31	17	24	11	14
Fade Margin (dB)	21	7	14	3*	6*
F_{FM} (dB)	24	24	21	24	23
SNR (dB)	62	48	52	42	44

* Includes use of threshold extender to reduce receiver threshold to 8 dB.

The half-power beam width of 2.1° does not provide adequate discrimination against signals from adjacent satellites spaced at 2°. (At the present time, however, the spacing between most adjacent satellites is greater than 2°.)

All of these performance criteria could be improved, while reducing the antenna size by the use of Ku band. The present commercial impediments to Ku band are described in Chapter 2.

Notes

1   EIA/TIA-250-C Standard, "Electrical Performance Standards for Television Transmission Systems," was issued January 4, 1990 and superseded RS-250-B. It can be ordered from the Electronic Industries Association, 2001 Pennsylvania Avenue, Washington, D.C. 20006.

2   Inglis, Andrew F., *Electronic Communications Handbook,* McGraw-Hill, New York, 1988.

6

FCC Rules and Procedures

6.1 OVERVIEW

6.1.1 Role and Authority of the FCC

The Federal Communications Commission (FCC) was established by the Communications Act of 1934, which gave it very broad authority to regulate interstate wired and wireless communications within the United States. Subsequently, the scope of its authority has been defined and broadened further by other statutes, among which was the Communications Satellite Act of 1962.

The regulation of satellite communications also requires international agreement. The International Telecommunications Union (ITU) governs radio services on an international level. It meets infrequently, and its year-to-year policy-making functions are handled by the World Administrative Radio Conference (WARC) and the Regional Administrative Radio Conference (RARC). To have the force of law, the decisions of these bodies must be specified in treaties that are ratified by the member countries.

Portions of the orbital arc have been allocated to the United States by treaty, and the FCC has the authority to assign orbital slots within these arc segments. Its policy for assigning slots was established by the *open skies* Order, which was issued in 1972. The policy states that any legally and financially qualified United States citizen or corporation is eligible to apply for a slot. It was an extremely important decision because, in contrast to previous practice, eligibility was not limited to existing common carriers. The financial resources required for the construction and launch of a satellite are large, greater than $100 million; and, in practice, this has limited satellite ownership to major corporations.

The procedures for the assignment of orbital slots is beyond the scope of this book, and this chapter is devoted to FCC Rules and procedures governing the installation and technical operation of uplink and downlink earth stations.

6.1.2 Deregulation

The open skies policy was the first major step in the FCC's steady progress in deregulating the satellite communications industry. Since then it has successively deregulated the nontechnical aspects of satellite communications, particularly the rates and conditions of lease or sale; and it removed the technical restrictions and mandatory licensing requirement for downlink receive-only earth stations. (The requirement for licensing uplink earth stations and the option of licensing downlink stations remain.) The salutary effect of deregulation on satellite service to the radio and television industries was described in Chapter 2.

6.1.3 FCC Rules and Regulations

The FCC's rules and regulations governing earth stations are contained in Part 25 of Title 47 of the Code of Federal Regulations. This can be downloaded from the National Archives and Records Administration Web site at:

http://www.access.gpo.gov/nara/

The rules concerning DBS stations are contained in the Final Acts of the 1983 Broadcast Satellite Service Regional Administrative Conference (RARC 1983). Among other provisions, this document specified the DBS orbital slots allocated to the United States and the maximum downlink power density.

6.2 TECHNICAL RULES

6.2.1 Uplink Earth Stations

The principal technical rules governing the operation of uplink earth stations have the purpose of minimizing interference to microwave receiving stations operating in the C band, 5925 to 6425 MHz. As a practical matter, no other services are authorized in the 14.0 to 14.5 GHz Ku uplink band.

There are four rules that address the interference problem: site requirements, Para. 25.203; power limits, Para. 25.204; minimum elevation angle, Para. 25.205; and antenna directivity, Para. 25.209.

6.2.1.1 Site Requirements

The FCC requires that a *coordination* procedure be carried out by the applicant for a new uplink earth station to demonstrate that harmful interference will not be caused to existing or authorized earth stations. The rules for coordination, described in Paras. 25.251 to 25.254, are complex and beyond the scope of this book, and applicants are advised to engage the services of a professional coordinator.

Certain preliminary actions can be taken before retaining a coordinator to screen out sites that clearly do not meet FCC requirements.

The first is to make field intensity measurements at the site over the complete frequency band—3700 to 4200 MHz for downlink stations and 5925 to 6425 MHz for uplinks. This will identify existing interference sources and also suggest the use of natural barriers for shielding.

The second is to consult with the Chief, Field Operations Bureau, Federal Communications Commission, Washington, D.C. 20554 if the proposed site is near an FCC monitoring station or a radio research facility operated by the Department of Defense or various civilian agencies.

The formal coordination process starts with the establishment of a *coordination distance,* defined as "... the distance within which there is a possibility of this earth station causing harmful interference to stations . . . sharing the same band . . ." This is initially assumed to be 100 km (Para. 25.251(d)(2). The coordinator then applies various criteria to evaluate the possibility of interference.

6.2.1.2 Power Limits

The uplink power limit applies only to "bands shared coequally with terrestrial communication services," that is, to C band, and only at elevation angles less than 5°. It varies from an EIRP of 40 dBW in any 4 kHz frequency band at the horizon to 55 dBW at an elevation angle of 5°. Since elevation angles less than 5° are not permitted except in unusual circumstances, this rule seldom applies.

6.2.1.3 Elevation Angle

Elevation angles of less than 5° for an uplink antenna are not ordinarily permitted because of potential interference to terrestrial circuits or possibly to adjacent satellites as the result of atmospheric scattering. Under special circumstances, the FCC may permit elevation angles between 3° and 5°. Under other circumstances it may require elevation angles greater than 5°. Aside from the FCC rule, it is usually bad practice in the Ku band to use an elevation angle less than 10° because of the long atmospheric path and severe rain attenuation.

6.2.1.4 Antenna Directivity

The FCC requirements for antenna directivity in the arc from 1° to 7° from the axis of the main lobe and in the plane of the geosynchronous arc as seen from the earth station are shown in Table 4.2. Requirements for directivity in other planes and in the arc beyond 7° are described in Para 25.209.

There is also an FCC requirement for off-axis cross-polarization isolation for C-band antennas. For off-axis angles, Θ, from 1.8° to 7°, the required isolation is:

Isolation (dBi) $= 19 - 25 \log \Theta$

For values of Θ from 7° to 9.2°, the required isolation is -2 dBi.

These values of isolation are in addition to those produced by the directivity of the antenna. Further, most satellite carriers have a requirement for on-axis polarization isolation, typically 30 dB.

6.2.2 Satellites

The FCC technical requirements for satellites that are of direct interest to users are the orbital spacing and the downlink power density limitation for C-band satellites.

Although some satellites are currently operating at spacings greater than 2°, the FCC's Rules and assignment policies are based on the assumption that all C-band and Ku-band satellites are spaced by 2°. DBS orbital slots are spaced by 9°.

The downlink power limitations apply only to C band and are described in Chapter 3.

6.2.3 Downlink Earth Stations

The original technical specifications for downlink earth stations were quite rigid. Since downlink stations do not cause interference, the primary purpose of the early specifications was to ensure high quality service. In the regulatory era, this was considered to be a legitimate role for the FCC. In the subsequent deregulatory era, it was considered more appropriate for the user to have the freedom to specify the service quality, particularly if the choice were between no service and service of lesser quality. It was also considered desirable for the cost/quality trade-off to be made by the marketplace rather than by a regulatory agency. As a result, the FCC eliminated the requirement for licensing downlink earth stations in 1979. The effect of this decision on the growth of the satellite communications industry was described in Chapter 2.

There remains, however, the need for protecting earth stations carrying high priority or high value traffic from interference from new stations. To provide this protection, the owner of a downlink station is given the option of obtaining a license. In return, a licensed station is required to meet strict technical standards with respect to site location, elevation angle, and antenna directivity.

6.2.3.1 Site Location

The applicant for a licensed downlink station must follow the same coordination procedure and meet the same interference standards as an uplink station. For downlink stations, of course, potential interference will be from transmitting stations rather than to receiving stations. As with uplink stations, interference from terrestrial sources should not be a problem in the Ku satellite band since no transmitters are licensed from 11.7 to 12.2 GHz.

6.2.3.2 Antenna Elevation Angle and Directivity

Downlink antennas should meet the same standards for elevation angle and directivity as uplinks. The FCC will assume that these standards are being met in calculating interference from new stations.

6.3 APPLICATION FOR EARTH STATION LICENSE

6.3.1 Procedure

An application for a construction permit should first be prepared on FCC Form 401: "Application for Authority to Construct and Operate a Proposed Earth Station." This form includes the information necessary for the FCC to act on the application for license, Form 403: "Application for Radio Station License or Modification Thereof under Parts 23 or 25."

6.3.2 Requirements

The applicant must be legally and financially qualified, and the proposed station must meet the technical requirements of Part 25 as described above. The application must include a complete coordination study, which demonstrates that the proposed facility will not result in objectionable mutual interference between the proposed station and existing or authorized terrestrial stations.

6.4 INTERNATIONAL SERVICE

Three types of international television service are now available:

1. The program source or destination is connected to an international gateway (see Chapter 2) by a terrestrial circuit or a United States satellite carrier. An earth station at the gateway accesses an Intelsat satellite, and the program is transmitted to or from a foreign *correspondent* facility by an Intelsat satellite. This service is ordered through Comsat, which makes all the arrangements and handles the scheduling.
2. Under certain conditions, United States earth stations other than those at the gateways can access Intelsat satellites directly. This saves the cost of the circuit to the gateway. This service is also ordered through Comsat.
3. After much controversy, two carriers were authorized to launch and operate satellites for international television service: PanAmSat to Latin America and Orion Satellite Corporation to Europe. Strict limits are placed on this service—most importantly that connection with public-switched telephone networks is forbidden, and that prior *consultation* with Intelsat is required to ensure that Intelsat will not suffer serious financial loss or *technical damage,* that is, excessive interference from the competing system.

7

Earth Station Operation and Maintenance

Many of the routine operational and maintenance procedures for earth stations are similar to those employed in other complex electronic systems. This chapter describes those that are unique to satellite systems.

7.1 SATELLITE OPERATION

7.1.1 Locating the Satellite

The first requirement for placing an earth station into operation, either as an uplink or a downlink, is to locate the satellite. This involves five steps, (1) calculating the satellite's elevation and azimuth as seen from the earth station's location, (2) preliminary aiming of the antenna in accordance with these calculations, (3) final aiming of the antenna by searching for the satellite in the vicinity of the calculated elevation and azimuth, (4) adjusting the antenna's polarization, and (5) verifying that the correct satellite has been located.

Locating the satellite must be done with more care for an uplink than a downlink because a transmission to the wrong satellite or on the wrong polarization or channel can cause serious interference to other satellite users. *One must be absolutely certain that the antenna is pointed at the correct satellite, that it is adjusted to the correct polarization, and that the exciter is tuned to the correct channel before the HPA is turned on.* In addition, a communication link should be established to a control center maintained by the satellite operator or resale carrier to verify that the aiming and polarization of the antenna, the tuning and adjustments of the exciter, and the adjustment of the HPA power are correct.

7.1.1.1 Calculating the Satellite's Azimuth and Elevation

The satellite's azimuth and elevation angles can be calculated by means of the equations in Appendix A.5 or by a calculator programmed for this purpose.

The variation in the angular location of the satellite within a limited area, say ±30 miles, is small—less than the error in aiming the antenna by compass and elevation indicator. A single set of calculated angles can be used by earth stations within this area, therefore, for the initial aiming of the antenna.

7.1.2 Preliminary Antenna Aiming

The antenna is first aimed in accordance with the calculated elevation and azimuth angles. The elevation is measured with an inclinometer and the azimuth with a compass. It is necessary, of course, to correct the compass reading with the local *variation,* the difference between true north and magnetic north. This can be obtained from U.S. Geological Survey maps or other sources. If the earth station is mobile, the truck is usually pointed to magnetic or true north by means of a compass and the azimuth of the antenna is measured with respect to the center line of the truck.

7.1.3 Final Antenna Aiming

Because of measurement inaccuracies, tropospheric bending, and the deviation of the earth from a perfectly spherical shape, it is unlikely that the initial aiming of the antenna on the basis of the calculated angles will be precisely accurate. For the final aiming of the antenna, the earth station is put in the receive mode and a small elevation-azimuth *box* around the calculated location is methodically scanned until a signal from the satellite is maximized. The receiver can be tuned either to a satellite beacon or to a transponder known to be operating on the satellite. This information can be obtained from the satellite operator or resale carrier.

7.1.4 Adjusting the Polarization

The polarization can be adjusted by tuning the receiver to an adjacent channel—which should be polarized at right angles—and rotating the antenna for *minimum* signal.

7.1.5 Verifying the Satellite

A spectrum analyzer is an invaluable tool in verifying that the correct satellite is being received. The 500 MHz spectrum of every satellite produces a characteristic *signature* on the analyzer that results from the types of traffic carried by its transponders. With the help of a listing of the traffic carried by each transponder, one can verify that the antenna is pointed at the desired satellite. With a little experience, it is possible to identify each satellite quickly.

7.2 UPLINK OPERATION

7.2.1 Exciter Adjustments

The uplink is the heart of the satellite transmission system because it determines the principle transmission parameters—the carrier frequency, the type of modulation, the modulation index for frequency-modulated systems, and the mode for transmitting the audio portion of the signal. The specific value of these parameters must be established by agreement between the satellite system licensee and the uplink and downlink operators.

7.2.1.1 Carrier Frequency

Each transponder has a designated frequency band, and the carrier frequency and all of its sidebands must fall within this band. If the transponder is shared by more than one carrier, for example, a second video channel or digital data channels, the satellite licensee will specify the frequency band to be occupied by each as well as its share of the transponder power.

A spectrum analyzer enables the operator to set both the carrier frequency and the modulation index (see discussion later in this chapter).

7.2.1.2 Modulation Index

In FM systems, the trade-off between SNR and fade margin that is involved in the selection of the modulation index is described in Section 5.4.1.2. Increasing the modulation index or peak-to-peak deviation improves the SNR but reduces the fade margin. The modulation index is also limited in transponders carrying more than one signal because it is necessary to limit the spectrum space occupied by the sidebands. Some *de facto* standards have been developed by the industry, although their use is not universal. They are as follows:

| | C band | Ku band | |
	1 Channel	1 Channel	2 Channels
Transponder bandwidth	40 MHz	54 MHz	54 MHz
IF bandwidth	36 MHz	36 MHz	24 MHz
p-p video deviation	21.5 MHz	21.5 MHz	18.2 MHz

An alternative for a two-channel Ku-band system is a p-p video deviation of 15 MHz and an IF bandwidth of 20 MHz.

The choice of the modulation index is a systems decision that should involve the customer, the uplink operator, the satellite operator, and the downlink operator.

The spectrum analyzer is used to measure the modulation index.

7.2.1.3 Energy Dispersal

An energy dispersal waveform (see Section 4.2.1.3) should be added to a video signal to be transmitted by a C-band satellite. This reduces the energy density per kHz in the downlink signal and increases the permissible downlink EIRP.

Again, the spectrum analyzer can be used to adjust the amount of frequency deviation introduced by the energy dispersal waveform.

7.2.1.4 Audio Subcarriers

The audio subcarrier frequencies and their modulation index should be set to the values established by the system design. Like the video modulation index, the choice of the audio subcarrier frequencies and their modulation index involves the customer, the uplink operator, the satellite operator, and the downlink operator.

The *de facto* standard for subcarrier frequencies are 6.2 and 6.8 MHz. A lower frequency such as 5.4 MHz is sometimes used to permit the use of a narrower bandwidth IF amplifier and a greater fade margin.

The FM broadcast deviation standard of ±75 kHz with the broadcast preemphasis standard is often used with satellites, although other standards are permissible. The ubiquitous spectrum analyzer can be used to adjust the frequency and modulation index of the audio subcarriers.

7.2.2 HPA Power Adjustment

The uplink operator should maintain communication with the satellite operator or the resale carrier control center while the uplink power is being adjusted. For multichannel transponders, the power should be set initially at a low level and adjusted upward so that it will not drive the transponder past saturation and adversely affect the performance of other channels.

7.3 DOWNLINK OPERATION

7.3.1 IF Bandwidth

Most receivers have variable bandwidth IF amplifiers. The bandwidth should be set to the narrowest bandwidth that accommodates all the significant sidebands in order to produce the largest fade margin. This can first be estimated by calculation and then determined empirically by reducing the bandwidth until the picture quality is significantly affected. (C-band systems operating with a large fade margin may use a somewhat wider bandwidth to produce the very best picture quality.) An approximate estimate of the bandwidth can be made from equation (7.1):

$$B_{IF} = 0.75[\Delta(f_v)] + 2SC_{AUDIO} \tag{7.1}$$

where:

B_{IF} is the IF bandwidth
$\Delta(f_v)$ is the peak-to-peak deviation
SC_{AUDIO} is the audio subcarrier frequency

7.3.2 Interfering Signals

Each channel in the C band should be checked for interfering signals from terrestrial microwave systems. As noted in Section 5.2, it may be possible to reduce or eliminate the interference by erection of obstacles or by installing trap filters in the IF amplifier at the location of the microwave carrier frequencies ±10 MHz from the center frequency of the satellite channel. This procedure should not be necessary, of course, at a site that has been cleared in accordance with FCC rules for licensed stations.

7.3.3 Measurement of CNR

The CNR is an important criterion of system performance, and it should be measured during installation of the link and periodically thereafter. It is measured in the receiver IF amplifier. (This measurement is sometimes erroneously described as a SNR measurement. Measuring SNR is more difficult and yields very little additional information on the operation of the system.)

Measuring the CNR requires a signal level meter that has been designed for this purpose. The signal level of a carrier operating at full power is first measured. The carrier power is then removed (or the receiver tuned to a nearby channel without power), and the noise power is measured. The difference in power levels is the CNR.

The measured value of CNR should then be compared with the value calculated with equation (5.1) and the cause of any major discrepancy determined.

7.3.4 Sun Outages

Sun outages are only a problem to downlink stations, and downlink station operators should ascertain the time and duration of the outages as described in Section 1.2.7. The only solution for these outages is to utilize a backup satellite that is far enough removed in the orbital arc to prevent overlap of the outage times. For point-to-point service, the decision to utilize a backup satellite is an economic one. Is the cost of the service interruption sufficient to warrant the cost of the temporary lease of a backup satellite? For point-to-multipoint service, there is the additional problem that the outage times are different for all downlinks, and every downlink station would have to install a second antenna. For service to broadcast network affiliates or cable TV program subscribers, the downlink stations should be advised of the outage times and the steps, if any, that have been taken by the uplink operator to provide backup service.

7.4 COMMUNICATION SUBSYSTEM

It is essential that the operator of an uplink earth station have facilities for constant communication with a satellite control center while it is being set up. After the system is in operation, a communication link must be available at all times to the control center and to the TV station or cable system master control. This is particularly critical for mobile earth stations that are moved frequently and that may not have access to a public telephone. Cellular telephone systems are usually available, and most mobile trucks also have facilities for communicating via the satellite on a small carrier or subcarrier. While not technically sophisticated, these systems are often complex, and operating personnel should become thoroughly acquainted with them before taking to the field.

7.5 MAINTENANCE

This section describes the special maintenance procedures that are unique to satellite earth stations.

7.5.1 SNR

The most critical performance criterion for a satellite system is its SNR, and a special maintenance program should be established to monitor this on a routine basis. The SNR is directly related to the CNR; and since CNR is more easily measured than SNR, it is more frequently used as the criterion of system performance.

CNR, measured as described earlier, should be compared with the value calculated by equation (5.1), and any major discrepancies should be investigated. The most likely causes of a below normal CNR are misalignment of the antenna or its components, or degradation of LNA performance; and the CNR measurement provides the most direct means of monitoring these system elements.

7.5.2 Linearity and Frequency Response

The linearity and frequency response of a complete earth station, including both an uplink and downlink, can be tested with a *loop test translator* without passing the signal through the satellite. The translator accepts a test signal at the output of the upconverter—in the range 5.925 to 6.425 GHz for C band or 14.0 to 14.5 GHz for Ku band—and translates it to the downlink frequency, 3.7 to 4.2 GHz for C band, or to a standard first IF frequency such as 950 to 1450 MHz. The signal then passes through the receiver downconverter, and the linearity and frequency response of the complete system are measured by standard techniques.

7.5.3 HPA Performance

The HPA is the uplink component that is most vulnerable to deterioration with age and usage, and the best criterion of its performance is the amount of drive required from the upconverter to produce the normal power output. If it becomes necessary to increase the HPA drive to produce the desired transponder drive—either to achieve saturation for a single channel or a predetermined power level for a multichannel transponder—it is a probable sign that the HPA is aging or that the antenna has become misaligned.

The antenna alignment should first be checked with the earth station in the receive mode, and if it is found to be correct, it is probable that the HPA is nearing the end of its life. If the station is carrying high-priority traffic, it would be advisable to replace the HPA. An even better solution is to employ two HPAs operated in parallel as described in Section 4.3.2.

7.6 SAFETY

7.6.1 General

It goes without saying that all of the safety standards published by the FCC, EIA, ANSI (American National Standards Institute), OSHA (Occupational Safety and Health Authority, United States Government), and other local and state government agencies should be followed meticulously. This is in addition to following the dictates of common sense. For example, care should be exercised to keep the area around an antenna clear when it is being rotated to aim it at another orbital slot.

7.6.2 Radiation Density

7.6.2.1 Standards

The radiation density safety standard that is applicable to uplinks requires special mention. It is based on the potential hazard that results from the very high level of electromagnetic power density in front of a highly directional uplink antenna. Unfortunately, there is not complete agreement on the power density level that is considered safe.

Microwave radiation is *nonionizing,* that is, unlike X-rays, for example, it does not ionize molecules that are exposed to it. The original standards for nonionizing radiation were based on the assumption that the only injurious effects were caused by heating of the tissues. On this basis, a limit of 10 mW/cm^2 was established by OSHA in 1983 (Standard 1910.17).

Some medical specialists believe, however, that long-term exposure to nonionizing radiation has other harmful effects, such as damage to the eyes, or, possibly, that it is carcinogenic. ANSI, the industry standardizing group, adopted a more stringent standard of 5mW/cm^2 (ANSI C95.1) in 1982. The issue was confused further by the adoption of an extremely rigid standard of 5 microwatts/cm^2 by the Soviet Union, although the evidence for this standard was very questionable. The ANSI standard is generally followed in the United States today.

7.6.2.2 Safe Distances

Because of the highly directional properties of satellite antennas, it is not difficult to avoid exposure to unsafe levels of radiation provided that one stays away from the center of the beam.

The distance to the 5 mW/cm^2 energy contour for an antenna having a gain of 48 dBi, an EIRP of 83 dBW at the beam center, and complying with the FCC directivity requirements of Table 4.2 are shown in the table below:

Angle from beam center	Distance to 5 mW/cm² contour
0°	565 m
>7°	<6 m*

The conclusion is that radiation from an uplink antenna is not a hazard, except at the beam center in the immediate vicinity of the antenna.

---

*   This calculation is only approximate because 6 meters is in the "near zone" of the antenna, and the pattern has not fully formed at this distance.

8

Satellite Services and Earth Station Equipment

8.1 OVERVIEW

This chapter describes the satellite services and earth station equipment that are available in the marketplace. The businesses of supplying these services and equipments are dynamic, and directories of suppliers are subject to frequent change. For up-to-date listings, the reader is referred to standard reference yearbooks that are updated annually. Two of these are the following:

> *Broadcasting & Cable Yearbook*
> R. R. Bowker, A Reed Reference Publishing Company
> 121 Chanlon Road
> New Providence, NJ 07974

and

> *Television and Cable Factbook*
> *Services Volume*
> Warren Publishing, Inc.
> 2115 Ward Court, N.W.
> Washington, D.C. 20037

8.2 SATELLITE SERVICES

Satellite services, that is, the right to use a satellite transponder, can be leased or purchased from a satellite *carrier* or from a *resale carrier*. Satellite carriers are licensed by the FCC to own and operate satellites and to offer satellite service for lease or sale. Resale carriers lease (or buy) earth and space segment facilities on a long-term basis and sublease them on a marked up, short-term basis. In effect it is a wholesale-retail relationship.

8.2.1 Satellite Carriers

There are presently three satellite carriers that sell or lease space segment facilities within the continental United States:

> AT&T
> Rts. 202-206
> Rm. 2A115W
> Bedminster, NJ 07921-0752

> GE American Communications, Inc.
> Four Research Way
> Princeton, NJ 08540

> Hughes Communications Inc.
> Box 92424
> Los Angeles, CA 90009

AT&T Alascom provides interstate and intrastate satellite service in Alaska:

> AT&T Alascom
> 210 E. Bluff Dr.
> Anchorage, AK 99502-1100

International television transmission services can be ordered through the Communications Satellite Corporation (Comsat) (see Chapter 2):

> Communications Satellite Corporation
> World Systems Division
> 950 L'Enfant Plaza S.W.
> Washington, D.C. 20024

8.2.2 Satellite Resale Carriers

Satellite resale carriers offer a number of useful services to the industry:

1. As described earlier, they fill the role of a wholesaler by leasing or buying satellite service on a long-term basis and subleasing it on a short-term basis to occasional users.
2. They act as systems integrators by providing network management for their customers and offering end-to-end service, employing a combination of satellite and terrestrial circuits.
3. In some cases they offer ancillary services such as recording program material for delayed transmission.

8.2.3 Site Coordination Services

The important role of site coordinators in obtaining earth station licenses was described in Chapter 6. Two site coordinators are the following:

> Jefa International
> Suite 280
> 1825 Plano Parkway
> Plano, TX 75074

and

> Comsearch
> 11720 Sunrise Valley Dr.
> Reston, VA 22091

8.2.4 Terms and Conditions of Lease and Sale

The satellite communications industry is now unregulated, and both satellite and resale carriers have responded to this highly competitive environment by offering satellite services under a wide variety of terms and conditions. They include different *grades* of service, *periods* of service, and *scope* of service. This includes the choice of leasing or buying either a complete satellite, a complete transponder, or a partial transponder.

8.2.4.1 Grades of Service

Three grades of satellite services are offered—*protected, unprotected,* and *preemptible.* The supplier of protected service provides a backup satellite and/or transponder so that service can be restored quickly in the event of failure of the protected transponder. Unprotected service has no backup facilities, but it cannot be preempted. Preemptible transponders are the backups for protected service, and they can be preempted if necessary. Preemptible service is much cheaper, and it is particularly appropriate for occasional service that otherwise would be very costly. Some full-time users to whom cost is most important also use preemptible service.

8.2.4.2 Periods of Service

Satellite service can be leased for time periods ranging from an hour to several years. Many satellite users do not have a long-term need for full-time communication facilities, and it is common practice for them to lease service on an *occasional* basis, either from a satellite or resale carrier. It can either be a long-term commitment for part time service, for example, two hours per day, or truly occasional service, as for SNG applications (see Chapter 2).

Since capital costs—amortization and capital return—are the major cost elements for the satellite companies, the hourly rate for a long-term lease with a guaranteed revenue stream can be much lower than the occasional hourly rate. The resale carrier takes advantage of this by obtaining a lower hourly rate in return for a commitment to a long term lease. He takes the risk that he will obtain enough occasional or *part time* business to meet his costs plus a profit.

8.2.4.3 Scope of Services

The scope of service offerings is broad, ranging from a portion of a transponder to a complete transponder with uplink and downlink services. The usage of part of a transponder is, of course, subject to strict technical limitations to avoid degradation of other circuits on the transponder.

8.2.4.4 Teleports

Teleports are now available in most major cities that have earth station facilities and interconnecting terrestrial links. These are available for lease to occasional users as required to complete their satellite circuits.

8.2.4.5 Transponder Sales

As the result of deregulation, space segment service can be purchased as well as leased. A full transponder or a part of a transponder, for example, for an SCPC circuit, can be purchased. Title to the purchased facilities passes to the customer, who has the right to use them full time, subject only to the technical rules of the FCC and the satellite carrier. The satellite carrier continues to operate the satellite bus for a lump-sum payment or an annual fee. The satellite carrier may also provide backup transponders that would be available for use in the event of failure of the primary transponders.

8.3 EARTH STATION EQUIPMENT

8.3.1 Overview

The rapid growth in the use of satellites for communications has led to an equal proliferation in the number of suppliers of earth station equipment and the scope of their offerings. The result is that an overwhelming variety of earth station equipment is now available in the marketplace. A systematic approach should be followed in selecting the items of equipment from this abundance that best meet the requirements of the application. Chapter 5 describes the basic factors involved in designing a system and selecting its equipment complement.

8.3.2 Consulting Services

An earth station customer may find it desirable to obtain consulting advice to assist in the design of the earth station installation. This can be obtained from a manufacturer, with the obvious drawback that his advice may not be completely objective, or from an independent consultant. The customer must make this choice. In either case, it will be advantageous for him to understand the system design process sufficiently to carry on an effective dialogue with the consultant.

8.3.3 Equipment Suppliers

This section provides a brief sampling of some of the leading suppliers of earth station equipment. It is not a complete list, but it is a starting point for the development of a bidders' list that would be appropriate for a particular requirement.

Antenna Suppliers
Andrew Corp.
10500 W. 153d St.
Orland Park, IL 60462

General Instrument Corporation
Jerrold Communications
2200 Byberry Road
Hatboro, PA 19040

Scientific-Atlanta, Inc.
4261 Communications Dr.
Norcross, GA 30093

LNAs, LNBs, and Receivers
Aventek, Inc.
481 Cottonwood Drive
Milpitas, CA 95035-7492

General Instrument Corporation
Jerrold Communications
2200 Byberry Road
Hatboro, PA 19040

LNR Communications, Inc.
180 Marcus Blvd.
Hauppage, NY 11788

Scientific-Atlanta, Inc.
4261 Communications Dr.
Norcross, GA 30093

Scramblers, Descramblers
General Instrument Corporation
Jerrold Division
2200 Byberry Road
Hatboro, PA 19040

Exciters, HPAs
Harris Corporation
Broadcast Division
Box 1487
3712 National Rd.
Richmond, IN 47375

Scientific-Atlanta, Inc.
4261 Communications Dr.
Norcross, GA 30093

Mobile Earth Stations
Satellite Transmission Systems Inc.
(Subsidiary of California Microwave Inc.)
125 Kennedy Drive
Hauppage, NY 11788

DBS Earth Stations
Hitachi
1-800-477-1212

Hughes Network Systems
1-800-274-8995

Magnavox
1-800-531-0039

Memorex
1-800-919-3647

Panasonic
1-888-726-2377

Sony
1-800-838-7669

Thomson Consumer Electronics
1-800-679-4776

Toshiba
1-800-867-4377

Appendix

A.1 CONVERSION OF FCC DOWNLINK POWER DENSITY LIMITS TO EIRP

The conversion of the FCC downlink power density limits (power per meter^2 per 4 kHz) to EIRP requires an assumption as to the distribution of carrier and side-band energy. For this purpose in FM systems, it is reasonable to assume that an energy dispersal waveform (see Section 4.2.1.3) superimposed on the video signal results in a uniform distribution of energy over a 2 MHz band at the center of the transponder pass band.

On the basis of this assumption, the maximum permissible C-band EIRP in terms of the FCC limit is the following:

$$\text{EIRP}_{\text{MAX}}\text{dBw} = [\text{FCC limit}]\text{dBw/m}^2/4\text{kHz} + 163 + 10 \log 2 \times 10^6 / 4 \times 10^3$$

A.2 ANTENNA DIRECTIVITY

The equations for calculating the half-power beam width (HPBW) and null beam width (angular separation of the nulls on either side of the main lobe) are the following:

$$\text{HPBW} = C_{\text{HP}}(\lambda/D)$$

$$\text{Null beam width} = C_{\text{null}}(\lambda/D)$$

where:

C_{HP} and C_{null} are constants which depend on the uniformity of reflector illumination.

For uniform illumination, $C_{\text{HP}} = 50°$ and $C_{\text{null}} = 114°$. For highly nonuniform illumination, $C_{\text{HP}} = 95°$ and $C_{\text{null}} = 280°$. For the examples in Table 4.1 which are typical of practical designs, $C_{\text{HP}} = 70°$ and $C_{\text{null}} = 170°$.

A.3 ANTENNA GAIN

The gain of an antenna with respect to an isotropic radiator expressed in decibels (dBi) is as follows:

$$\text{Gain} = 10 \log([4.1 \times 10^4][E]/[HPBW_1][HPBW_2]) \text{ dBi}$$

where:

E is the antenna efficiency. Antenna efficiencies range from 50 to 85 percent. For the examples in Table 4.1, which are typical of practical designs, an efficiency of 70 percent was assumed.

$HPBW_1$ and $HPBW_2$ are the half-power beam widths in orthogonal planes in degrees. For a circular antenna with a symmetrical pattern, this factor becomes $[HPBW]^2$.

A.4 NOISE TEMPERATURE

The equation relating thermal noise power to temperature is the following:

$$\text{Noise power} = kBT$$

where:

k is the Boltzman constant = 1.38×10^{-23} Joules/K°/Hz
B is the bandwidth in Hertz
T is the absolute temperature in degrees Kelvin

$$T_{Kelvin} = T_{Centigrade} + 273°.$$

A.5 ANTENNA ELEVATION AND AZIMUTH ANGLES

To determine the elevation and azimuth angles of the path to a geosynchronous satellite, first calculate the angle, β, and the path length, L:

$$\beta = \cos^{-1}(\cos[\Delta\ long]\cos[lat])$$

Where:

[Δ long] is the difference between the longitudes of the earth station and the satellite and [lat] is the earth station latitude.

$$L = (18.2 - 5.4\cos[\beta]) \times 10^4 \text{ km.}$$

(L varies from 35,800 km with the satellite directly overhead to 39,550 km at an elevation angle of 10°.)

The elevation angle is then given by the equation:

$$\text{Elevation angle} = \cos^{-1}(4.22 \times 10^4 / L)(\sin[\beta])$$

and the azimuth angle is given by the equation:

$$\text{Azimuth} = (180° + \tan^{-1}(\tan[\Delta\ long]/\sin[lat])$$

Glossary

ad hoc network A television or radio network that is formed for a limited period of time to cover a specific event, for example, a major sports contest.

ADC Analog-to-digital conversion. The process of converting analog audio or video signals into a stream of digital data. See *DAC*.

ADDS Audio digital distribution service. Also called DATS (digital audio transmission service). A system for the distribution of radio programs by satellite, using a digital signal.

ADPCM Adaptive differential pulse-code modulation. A digital compression technique that is sometimes used for audio signals.

AKM Apogee kick motor. An explosive charge in the satellite that provides the energy for the final stage of the launch and places the satellite in the geosynchronous orbit.

B-MAC Multiplexed analog components, type B. A format for the transmission of color television programs with three separate signals using analog time-division multiplexing. This is in contrast to the multiplexed NTSC and PAL systems that transmit the color information with a high-frequency subcarrier.

Backyard dish A low-cost TVRO designed for home use.

baseband The voice, video, audio, or data signal transmitted by a communication system.

beacon A small transmitter installed on a satellite that transmits continuously. It is used for aiming earth station antennas and automatic power level control for Ku-band uplinks.

bus See Space vehicle.

C band A portion of the radio frequency spectrum. Communication satellites are allocated C-band frequencies from 5.925 to 6.425 GHz for uplinks and 3.700 to 4.200 GHz for downlinks.

Cassegrain antenna A dual reflector antenna in which the subreflector is convex toward the main reflector.

CCIR An international standards body that is now part of the International Telecommunication Union (ITU). See ITU.

Cleared site An earth station site that is free from interference by microwave systems and other earth stations.

CNR Carrier-to-noise ratio. The ratio of the signal level at the input of a receiver to the receiver's noise level referred to the input.

Communications Satellite Act of 1962 An Act of Congress that delegated authority for the regulation of communications satellites to the Federal Communications Commission (FCC).

compression In digital systems, the process of modifying a video or audio data stream to reduce the data rate without noticeably impairing the signal performance.

Comsat Communications Satellite Corporation. A private company formed in 1962 pursuant to the Communications Satellite Act. It is the chosen instrument of the United States to hold this country's interest in Intelsat, and to operate the United States ground segment of the Intelsat system.

coordination A term applied to the site selection process required by the FCC to make sure that an earth station on the site will neither cause nor receive excessive interference from existing stations.

cross-strapping Interconnecting C-band and Ku-band transponders on a hybrid satellite so that the uplink is in one band and the downlink in the other.

DAC Digital-to-analog conversion. The process of converting digital data into analog audio or video signals.

DATS Digital audio transmission service. Also called ADDS (digital audio transmission service). A system for the distribution of radio programs by satellite, using digital signals.

DBS Direct broadcast by satellite. A system of television program distribution in which programs are transmitted direct from a satellite to homes. In its specialized usage, the term applies to very high-power satellites that permit reception with very small antennas.

DBS Authorization Center A facility established by the General Instrument Corporation in La Jolla, California, to provide backyard dishes with authorization codes to descramble programs.

DCT Discrete cosing transform. A video compression technique.

deemphasis See preemphasis.

digital Pertaining to systems that transmit signals as a series of discrete values. The most common digital format is *binary*, which represents signals in a stream of *bits*, having only two values: 0 or 1.

downconverter A satellite receiver component that translates the high-frequency carriers of a group of channels (or of a single channel) downward to an intermediate frequency for amplification.

downlink A radio-transmission circuit from satellite to earth station.

dual-reflector antenna An antenna consisting of a parabolic reflector that is illuminated by reflected energy from a subreflector.

earth station An installation for the transmission and/or reception of signals to and from a satellite.

EIA Electronic Industries Association. The major trade association of electronic manufacturers in the United States.

EIRP Effective isotropic radiated power. The ratio, expressed in decibels, between the radiated power density and the power density radiated by a 1-watt transmitter from an isoptropic radiator.

elevation-over-azimuth mount An antenna mounting system in which the elevation and azimuth angles are adjusted independently.

ENG Electronic news gathering. A system of television journalism in which live pictures of news events are recorded on tape or transmitted from the scene to the station by electronic means, usually microwave or satellite. See *SNG*.

error protection In digital systems, the process of inserting redundancy into a data stream so that subsequent transmission errors may be detected and corrected.

fade margin The ratio of the carrier-to-noise level in a receiver under normal operating conditions to the receiver threshold.

Faraday effect The rotation of the plane of polarization of a radio wave when subjected to a strong magnetic field.

ferrite polarizer A device for rotating the plane of polarization of a radio wave by the use of the Faraday effect.

field effect transistor A type of transistor with a very low noise temperature, frequently used in the input stage of satellite receivers.

FM Frequency modulation. A transmission method where signals modulate the frequency of a carrier.

FM improvement factor The ratio, expressed in decibels, between the SNR in the demodulated output of a frequency modulated carrier and the CNR.

footprint The area on the surface of the earth that receives a signal of useful strength from a satellite.

frequency reuse Doubling the channel capacity of a satellite by the use of cross polarization.

FSS Fixed service satellites. Satellites used for communication services that are neither broadcast nor mobile.

G/T In an earth station receiving system, the ratio of the antenna gain to the receiver noise temperature. It is a fundamental figure of merit for a receiving system.

geosynchronous orbit A circle 22,300 miles above the earth in the equatorial plane. The centrifugal force and the force of gravity on an object in this orbit are exactly balanced when it rotates in synchronism with the earth.

geosynchronous satellites Satellites located in the geosynchronous orbit.

Gregorian antenna A dual-reflector antenna in which the subreflector is concave toward the main reflector.

Gregux antenna A dual-reflector antenna in which the subreflector is a concave ring.

ground segment The terrestrial portion of a satellite communication system, that is, its earth stations.

half-power beam width (HPBW) The angle between the points on the main lobe of an antenna beam where the radiated power density is one-half that at the peak of the lobe.

HPA High-powered amplifier. The final amplifier in an uplink transmitter.

hybrid satellites Satellites having both K-band and C-band transponders.

Intelsat International Telecommunications Satellite Consortium. An international organization that owns and operates the satellites used for international satellite communication services.

ISO International Organization for Standardization.

isotropic radiator A hypothetical antenna that radiates equally in all directions.

ITU International Telecommunication Union. An international regulatory body that has been delegated the authority to establish policies in international communication matters. This includes the allocation of orbital slots to the countries of the world. The ITU subsumes the activities of former CCIR and CCITT organizations.

Ku band A portion of the radio frequency spectrum. Communication satellites are allocated Ku-band frequencies from 14.0 to 14.5 MHz for uplinks and 12.2 to 12.7 GHZ for dowlinks. DBS satellites are allocated Ku-band frequencies from 17.3 to 17.8 GHz for uplinks and 12.2 to 12.7 GHz for downlinks.

LNA Low-noise amplifier. The initial amplifying stage in an earth station receiver designed to generate very little noise.

LNB Low-noise block converter. A component that combines the functions of a *LNA* and a *downconverter.*

look angle The angle above the horizontal of a satellite as seen from a point on the earth. Also called *elevation angle.*

loop test translator A unit of test equipment that simulates the uplink/downlink frequency conversion in a satellite so that a complete earth station can be tested without using a satellite.

magnetic variation The angle at a point on the earth's surface between magnetic north and true north.

modulation index In an FM system, the ratio of the frequency deviation to the highest modulating frequency.

MPEG Motion Picture Expert Group. A committee of the ISO that developed the video compression methods that are called MPEG.

noise Broadly, a term used to describe any unwanted electrical disturbance in a communication signal. Specifically, a term used to describe a random disturbance caused by thermal effects (thermal noise) or similar in nature to thermal noise but not of thermal origin. The visual effect of thermal noise in a video signal is a *snowy* picture; in a radio signal it produces *hiss.*

noise temperature A criterion for specifying the electrical noise power generated by a system component or a complete system. It is defined as the temperature at which a hot object would generate or emit the same amount of thermal noise power.

nonionizing radiation Radiation, for example, satellite transmissions, that does not ionize molecules that are exposed to it. This distinguishes it from ionizing radiation such as X-rays.

NRTC The National Rural Telecommunication Co-op. A third patty (controlled neither by cable TV operators nor program suppliers) organization that was formed to receive orders from the public for scrambled pay-TV services and to inform the appropriate authorization center.

NTSC National Television Systems Committee. An *ad hoc* committee convened from time to time by the National Association of Broadcasters and the Electronic Industries Association to study and recommend television standards and specifications.

NTSC color system The system developed by the NTSC in 1952 and later approved by the FCC for color broadcasting in the United States.

open skies policy A policy announced in an Order issued by the FCC in 1972 stating that any legally and financially qualified United States citizen or corporation could apply for and be granted an orbital slot.

orbital slot A fixed location in the geosynchronous orbit that is assigned by regulatory authorities to a specific satellite.

packetizing In a digital data-transmission system, a method that divides data into separate blocks (packets) for transmission. By interleaving packets, multiple data streams can be multiplexed on the same circuit.

PAL color system Phase alternating lines. A color system, which is a variant of the NTSC system, that is used widely in Europe.

parametric amplifier A type of amplifier with a very low noise temperature, frequently used in the input stage of satellite receivers.

payload The communication system components in a satellite.

pixel A single point of a video image, having independent brightness and color parameters.

pointing accuracy The rms angular deflection of an antenna, measured over a period of time, at stated levels of wind velocity.

polar mount An antenna mounting system in which the antenna is rotated around an axis that is parallel to the earth's axis.

preemphasis Enhanced amplification of the higher frequency components of video and audio signals before transmission. An inverse function, *deemphasis*, at the receiver improves the SNR.

preemptible service Unprotected satellite service that can be preempted by services of higher grade.

prime orbital arcs The portion of the geosynchronous orbit in which the look angle exceeds 5° for C band or 10° for Ku band in the desired service area.

prime-focus-feed antenna An antenna consisting of a parabolic reflector that is illuminated directly with a feed horn located at its focus.

program syndicators Independent entrepreneurs who obtain the rights to resell television programs to broadcasters.

protected service Satellite service provided with back-up facilities that can be used to continue service in the event of a satellite or transponder failure.

PSK Phase shift keying. A modulation mode for the transmission of digital signals. It reverses the phase of a carrier based on the binary digital values of 0 or 1.

QPSK Quaternary phase shift keying. A version of PSK that uses four phases of a carrier to transmit two bits of binary digital data at a time.

RARC Regional Administrative Radio Conference. A conference at which the policy making functions of the ITU for matters of interest to a single region are exercised.

receiver threshold The CNR below which the performance of a receiver's detection circuits (FM or digital) deteriorate rapidly.

resale carrier An organization that leases communication facilities on a long-term wholesale basis and subleases them on a short-term retail basis.

scrambling The deliberate distortion of video and/or audio signals to prevent their reception by unauthorized viewers.

sideband energy dispersal The spreading of the sideband energy from a frequency modulated carrier over an area of the spectrum to reduce the energy density expressed in watts per kHz of bandwidth.

site coordinator A consultant who performs the earth station site coordination functions required by the FCC for new sites.

SNG Satellite news gathering. A form of ENG that uses satellite communication.

solar eclipse The time interval when the earth comes between the sun and the satellite, thus making solar energy unavailable at the satellite.

space segment The portion of a satellite communication system located in space, i.e., the satellite.

space shuttle A reusable launch vehicle that carries satellites to an elevation of about 200 miles and then returns to earth.

space vehicle The housing, electrical, and mechanical systems of the satellite that provide *station keeping* and a working environment for the payload. This is also called the *bus*.

specialized network A network with programming that is regional or that has specialized content.

spectrum analyzer A type of test equipment that displays the amplitude of signal frequency components in an entire region of the spectrum.

spin-stabilized satellites Satellites whose orientation is controlled by spinning the entire housing.

SSPA Solid state power amplifier. A high-power amplifier employing solid state components.

station keeping The process of maintaining a satellite in its assigned orbital slot and in the proper orientation relative to the earth.

sun outage The blocking of a downlink signal as the result of excessive solar noise in the receiver when the satellite and sun are in line as seen from the earth station.

teleport A major earth station installation having terrestrial interconnections and extensive facilities for accessing a number of satellites.

three-axis-stabilized satellites Satellites whose attitude is controlled by internal gyroscopes. See spin-stabilized satellites.

torus antenna A multiple-beam antenna in which the reflecting surface is circular in the plane of the feed horns and parabolic in the plane orthogonal to the feed horns.

transponder An electronic component of a satellite that shifts the frequency of an uplink signal and amplifies it for retransmission to the earth in a downlink.

TT&C An earth station used for tracking, telemetry, and control of satellites in orbit.

TVRO Television, receive only. An earth station designed for downlink service only.

TWTA Travelling wave tube amplifier. A device for generating comparatively large amounts of power in the microwave regions of the spectrum.

unprotected service Satellite service with no backup facilities. Unprotected service, however, cannot be preempted.

upconverter A component of an uplink earth station that translates the intermediate-frequency carriers of a group of channels (or of a single channel) upward to the final carrier frequency.

uplink A radio-transmission circuit from earth station to satellite.

VideoCipher The trade name for a scrambling system manufactured by the General Instrument Corporation. It has become the *de facto* scrambling standard for cable TV programs. (VideoCipher is a registered trademark of the General Instrument Corporation.)

VSAT Very small aperture terminals. Small earth stations, antenna diameter approximately 1.8 meters, used for transmission of digital signals at a 56 or 64 kbs rate. Can be used for teleconferencing.

WARC World Administrative Radio Conference. A conference that exercises the policy-making functions of the ITU for matters of worldwide interest.

weighted noise The noise power in a circuit or system calculated by weighting its frequency components in proportion to their visibility for video signals and audibility for audio signals.

Bibliography

REFERENCE BOOKS

Baylin, F., *World Satellite Yearly*. Boulder, CO: Baylin Publications, annual.

Benson, K. B., and J. Whitaker, *Television Engineering Handbook*. New York: McGraw-Hill, 1992.

British Broadcasting Corporation. *Handbook*. London: BBC, annual.

Broadcasting & Cable Yearbook, R. R. Bowker, A Reed Reference Publishing Company, New Providence, NJ, annual.

Dorf, R. C., *The Electrical Engineering Handbook*. Boca Raton: CRC Press, 1993.

Fink, Donald G., and Donald Christiansen, *Electronic Engineers Handbook*. 3d Ed. New York: McGraw-Hill, 1989.

Gibson, J. D., *The Communications Handbook*. Boca Raton: CRC Press, 1997.

Inglis, Andrew F., *Electronic Communications Handbook*. New York: McGraw-Hill, 1988.

Television & Cable Factbook: Cable & Services Volume. Washington, D.C.: Warren Publishing Inc., annual.

TECHNICAL BOOKS

Barlett, Eugene R., *Cable Television Technology and Operations*. New York: McGraw-Hill, 1990.

Baylin, F., *Miniature Satellite Dishes*. Boulder, CO: Baylin Publications, 1994.

Elbert, B. R., *The Satellite Communication Application Handbook*. Boston: Artech House, 1997.

Ha, Tri T., *Digital Satellite Communications,* 2nd Ed. New York: McGraw-Hill, 1990.

Inglis, A. F., and Luther, A. C., *Video Engineering*, 2nd Ed. New York: McGraw-Hill, 1997.

Luther, A. C., *Principles of Digital Audio and Video*, Boston: Artech House, 1997.

Magnant, Robert S., *Domestic Satellites: An FCC Giant Step Toward Competitive Communications*. Boulder, CO: Westview Press, 1977.

Miya, K. *Satellite Communications Technology*. Tokyo: KDD Engineering and Consulting, Inc., 1981.

Roddy, D., *Satellite Communications*, 2nd Ed. New York: McGraw-Hill, 1996.

Watkinson, John, *The Art of Digital Video,* 2nd Ed. Boston: Focal Press, 1994.

STANDARDS AND RECOMMENDATIONS

ITU Recommendations and Reports, available online at http://www.itu.ch.

EIA Standards, EIA Engineering Department, Washington, D.C.; especially:

    EIA/TIA-250-C Video performance standards

    EIA/TIA-250-C Audio performance standards

REGULATORY

FCC Rules and Regulations, Satellite Communications, Title 47, Part 25 of the Code of Federal Regulations. Government Printing Office, Washington, D.C. Available online at http://www.access.gpo.gov/nara/index.html.

Index

Focal Press

Focal Press

Related Title

Commercial Satellite Communications

by Stephan C. Pascall and David Withers

This book contains the most up-to-date technology and covers the many facets of satellite communications–from the design of the radio link to the technology used within the orbiting satellite and the construction of the satellite base station. These aspects are described and illustrated by reference to the various satellites currently in use or planned to be launched.

Contents

Part One: Introduction • Part Two: Platforms in Space • Launchers and Launching • Satellite Technology • Part Three: Satellite Communications Technology • Control of Radio Interference • Analogue Transmission • Digital Transmission • Part Four: Applications for Satellite Communications • Domestic Public Networks and Private Systems • VSAT Networks in the FSS • Satellite Communications for Mobile Earth Stations • Satellite Broadcasting

Stephan C. Pascall is Principal Administrator for the Commission of European Communities. He has worked for many years with BT.

David Withers is a consultant in Satellite Communication.

June 1997 • 512pp • Hardback • 0-7506-1235-5 • $114.95

Available from all better book stores or in case of difficulty call:
1-800-366-2665 in the U.S. or +44 1865 310366 in Europe.

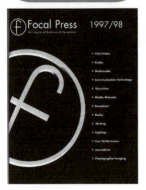